ON BRITAIN

ON BRITAIN
RALF DAHRENDORF

The University of Chicago Press

941.085
D131.
1982

The University of Chicago Press, Chicago 60637
British Broadcasting Corporation, London W1M 4AA

© 1982 by Ralf Dahrendorf

89 88 87 86 85 84 83 82 54321

Library of Congress Cataloging in Publication Data

Dahrendorf, Ralf
  On Britain

  Bibliography: p.
  1. Great Britain – Economic conditions – 20th century.
  2. Great Britain – Social conditions – 20th century
  3. Great Britain – Politics and government – 20th century
  4. National characteristics, British.   I. Title.
  HC256.D33   1982   941.085'8   82-60102
  ISBN 0-226-1340-5 (pbk.)

CONTENTS

1 A Personal Preface   9

A CENTURY OF DECLINE

2 Decline Without Fall   18
3 The Strengths of Weakness, the Weaknesses of Strength   24
4 Decline and (Almost) Fall   33

CLASS, AND OTHER ATTITUDES

5 The Vanishing of the Industrial Spirit   42
6 A Matter of Inequality?   51
7 The Upper Classes, or How the Tone is Set   55
8 The Working Classes, or How Things Hold Together   62
9 Does Class Matter?   73

WESTMINSTER, AND OTHER INSTITUTIONS

10 A Place of Strife   80
11 The Westminster Game   87
12 Short-term thinking   93
13 A Corporate Bias   98
14 London and the Rest   104
15 The Politics of Economic Decline   110
16 Some Steps Forward   115

EUROPE, AND OTHER LINKS WITH THE WORLD

17 A Question of Identity   128
18 Post-Imperial Britain   135
19 Special Relationships   139
20 The European Dilemma   145

A FUTURE THAT MIGHT WORK

21 Britain in the 1980's   156
22 Models of Britain   162
23 The Economy, or Which Future Works   173
24 A British Future   181

Notes   189

ON BRITAIN

Chapter One
A PERSONAL PREFACE

For the young German, armed with a 'Temporary Travel Document' issued by the Military Government, an 'Exit Permit', a 'Re-Entry Permit', and above all the entry visa to the United Kingdom, the train trip to the Hook of Holland was a source of great excitement. I was eighteen; it was January, 1948, and the War was still very much on most English people's minds, especially when they met a German. However, neither this nor the stormy Channel night in the bowels of a military transporter could dampen the excitement: England, at last! ('When people say England,' George Mikes notes in *How to Be an Alien*, 'they sometimes mean Great Britain, sometimes the United Kingdom, sometimes the British Isles – but never England'.[1] The same is true for this book.) England began with one of those legendary breakfasts on the Boat Train from Harwich to Liverpool Street. Then we were taken across London and out again from Marylebone Station to Beaconsfield, or more precisely, to Wilton Park, where German PoWs and groups of Germans like ours spent six weeks being 're-educated'.

This was not my first contact with the country with which I had fallen in love even before I first saw it. There were, for example, the officers of the occupation army who looked after young Germans, invited them to their homes, arranged discussion evenings, and gave them cigarettes and even an occasional gin and tonic. Some of them were, and are, famous, such as the great Sir Robert Birley, who has done more for liberty in a practical and personal way than anyone else I ever met. Others remained uncelebrated, but did their part: Major Wolsey, Captain Luxton – they are now back wherever they came from, but they did more than could be expected of an officer of an occupation army. They represented the best of Britain.

Then, before my time, as it were, there had been my mother's long-planned visit to England which was never to take place. In the mid 1920s, she, a young secretary in Hamburg, had saved up money and made careful preparations, when blood poisoning in a finger forced her to abandon the trip at the last minute. Instead, she went to a small place outside Hamburg, in what is called 'Hostein Switzerland', and there she met my father. My parents decided, as a modest substitute for the abortive trip, to give their children names which would be useable equally in Germany and in Britain. My brother's name is Frank.

Hamburg, of course, is in any case the most English city in Germany. In fact, it is far more English than any place in the British Isles. Somehow, people's pin-striped suits are more pin-striped than those of the City of London, and their reserved coolness is, unlike the British, real. I was born in Hamburg, as were both my parents. All my grandparents had come to Hamburg from that much fought-over strip of land between Germany and Denmark which is called Anglia, and from which the Anglo-Saxons may have come – whatever this proves so far as my English credentials are concerned.

Shortly before the end of the Wilton Park weeks, I fell ill with severe tonsillitis. To my initial dismay I was taken to Amersham General Hospital. However, the ten days in the general ward soon turned out to be the most important of the whole trip. (I was to write a broadcast about them, still in 1948, which described England 'From the Bed Perspective'.[2]) There was first of all the kindness of Larry and John and Tim and Cato and the others who gave me freely of their (still rationed) goodies. Then there were the many conversations about Germany: 'Why did we have to go to war against each other?' and: 'We English like people who help themselves. If you Germans try to help yourselves, we will happily help you.' Larry proudly showed me his razor 'made in Germany'; Tim was disappointed that I did not know the woman in the tiny place in the Rhineland to whom he had sent a parcel at Christmas. Then there was the kindness and ease of life in the ward, an enveloping sense of community. I had no visitors on visitors' day, but they would never let me even realise the fact. And, of course, there were many personal chats. When Cato and I shared the grapes which his wife had brought him, he praised his wife, 'the best woman in the world', and went on to tell me of his work, the fun they had in going to the races, or to a soccer game, and said that life was really quite good. Did he want to get on, advance, have a career? His answer was straight and without qualification: 'Why? I am quite happy. The gentry have their life. We have nothing to do with it. And we have our life, which is none of their business.'

George Mikes's *How to Be an Alien* had already been published by then. I was not yet a resident alien, but I loved the book. Remember how Mikes describes the 'national passion' for queuing? 'At weekends an Englishman queues at the bus-stop, travels out to Richmond, queues up for a boat, then queues up for tea, then queues up for ice-cream, then joins a few more odd queues for the sake of the fun of it, then queues up at the bus-stop, and has the time of his life.'[3] Things have changed since then. This book is above all about changes. Yet in all change some things remain the same. The *New Standard* published two pictures of a woman who first, after the riots in Toxteth, Liverpool, in July 1981, stood in a queue outside a large shop window which had been smashed by rioting youths, and in the second picture could be seen staggering home under a load of looted goods.

The next time I came to England was with somewhat more serious intent. In 1952 I had, at the tender age of twenty-two, completed my doctorate in philosophy at the University of Hamburg. Since this was, at least by Continental standards, an absurdly early age to do anything, I somehow had to 'lose' a year or two. I knew that I wanted to find out something about society (which was not, then, so fashionable as it was to become a decade later); I also knew that I wanted to go back to England – and I had vaguely heard of a place called the London School of Economics. Thus, by September 1952, I found myself a postgraduate in sociology at LSE.

One may doubt whether LSE is a typically British institution, but there is little doubt that it is an institution which can exist only in Britain. The very internationalism of this academic universe betrays the tradition of a country whose people, values, and institutions had spread all over the world. While the Empire was beginning to turn into the more tenuous Commonwealth, the London School of Economics and Political Science remained a place in which Nigerians and Americans, Malaysians and Jamaicans, Mauritians and even Germans met. Of the academic greatness of the place there is no need to talk in this context. Nor is this the place to describe its departments, its library, or even its style in any detail. Physically, LSE is a cramped and rough place, located as it is in the centre of London. Not everybody finds it possible to stand the noise, the pace, the pressure which surrounds it. LSE is also a place which leaves its students to their own resources; though if they have them, they can learn as much from each other as from any of their teachers. But above all, LSE is a great paradox, a paradox of purity and commitment, of detachment and involvement. It is this paradox which has given rise to so many of the misunderstandings, or half-understandings of what its friends affectionately call 'the School'.

The institution of LSE is politically neither 'left' nor 'right'. People enjoyed listening to Harold Laski (who died before I came), but they compensated for the fun by going to the other professor of politics, K. B. Smellie, in order to learn something. In any case, Lionel Robbins and Friedrich von Hayek were hardly economists of the Left. But, more important, the institution as such has always stayed clear of politics. There is the moving statement in which the founder of LSE, Sidney Webb, himself of course a lifelong Fabian, and Labour politician, reports his reply to an early charge by someone that the LSE was in fact a breeding ground of socialism: 'I said that, as he knew, I was a person of decided views, Radical and socialist, and that I wanted the policy that I believed in to prevail. But that I was also a profound believer in knowledge and science and truth. I thought that we were suffering much from lack of research in social matters, and that I wanted to promote it. I believed that research and new discoveries would prove some, at any rate, of my views of policy to be right, but that, if they proved the contrary, I should cheerfully abandon my own policy. I think that is a fair attitude.'[4]

At the same time, members of LSE have always had their personal political commitments. Sidney Webb and Harold Laski, or Lionel Robbins and Friedrich von Hayek, are but examples. The first two Directors of LSE, W. A. C. Hewins, and Halford McKinder, had been conservative MPs. William Beveridge, Director for nearly twenty years, was both a liberal and one of the founders of the welfare state. But somehow such personal involvement did not spill over into the institution. And thus it was a great place for a young man who himself believed as strongly in the asceticism of scholarship as in the need to take part in the effort to maintain and advance liberty.

In those years, England was still very much a country which combined average economic progress with considerable social strength. There will be more to say about this later. My own means being modest – and Germany at that time still lagging behind Britain – I did not mind much about the slow pace of economic growth. The other side of life was all the more enjoyable: the warmth of human relationships, the seemingly endless chats in pubs or digs about all and sundry, the occasional forays by Green Line bus into the countryside. In connection with my dissertation on 'Unskilled Labour in British Industry', I travelled North, visited factories, talked to personnel officers and to shop stewards. The unskilled then seemed a kind of underclass, less involved in industrial conflict than the semi-skilled and the skilled. Still, the experience somehow led me along a path which was to end in an understanding of a kind of conflict which is very British indeed: conflict as a zero-sum game in which one either wins or loses, and one side has to lose what the other wins. Conflict as a cup game, one might say, where in the end there cannot be a draw. I did not notice at the time, surrounded as I was by 'scholarship boys' and 'aliens', that my interest in football – I transferred my loyalty from SV Hamburg to Arsenal London – was out of keeping with the expectations of some. I knew of course that conflict had to do with class, but the full weight of class in Britain only dawned on me later. The years from 1952 to 1954 were rich and rewarding. When I left, I left with sadness.

The following twenty years were, for me, German years, leavened by some America, a little Italy, and occasional visits to Britain. As a member of the Commission of the European Communities in the early 1970s, I followed Britain's negotiations for entry into the EEC closely. My colleague Jean-François Deniau, the chief negotiator for the EEC, sat next to me at the big round Commission table in Brussels and let me watch the ups and downs of the talks. It was a tense negotiation, from the first day on which the British Government declared that it would accept the principles of the Common Agricultural Policy, to the final day when a woman threw an ink bag at Prime Minister Heath as he was coming up the steps of the Palais Egmont to sign the act of accession. Naturally, I wanted Britain in Europe; at the same time, I had already come to the conclusion that there was a worrying discrepancy between the needs of Europe and the reality of the European Communities. This meant that there was a discrepancy also between the political intentions of the British Government, and the economic realities of the EEC. Deniau knew this, as did Raymond Barre. Some in Britain must have felt it, though the misplaced enthusiasm of both defenders and attackers of the EEC soon came to make it difficult to have a rational discussion of things European at all. This is true to the present day, and so I am bound to be misunderstood if I say that in my view Britain is a European country, whatever its other ties and obligations may be; that Britain must be a part of any serious European venture; but that in 1973, the price for the particular venture called European Communities had become very high. Unless it is lowered, both Britain and Europe will suffer.

However, Britain joined. My new Commission portfolio brought me into contact with the British Secretary of State for Education and Science, Margaret Thatcher (as well, of course, as the other eight ministers of education). But my enthusiasm for Europe did not grow. Years earlier, in 1971, I had written, pseudonymously, a series of articles taking the European Community to task.[5] At the time, I was severely criticised by my colleagues as well as praised by false friends. During a tense hour of the European Parliament, a motion of censure was narrowly avoided.[6] But in 1973, more and more people, real friends, came up to me to assure me that I had been entirely right. Disillusionment spread in Brussels and in the capitals. Lord Robbins therefore chose the right psychological moment when, in the summer of 1973, he invited me to lunch and asked me whether I would be prepared to accept the Directorship of the London School of Economics from October 1974 for a period of ten years.

I accepted, and thus finally became a resident alien in Britain, with a work permit but no vote. Actually, I have never felt hemmed in. Immigration from Commonwealth countries apart (and this is a serious and sad story), Britain has been like Ancient Rome: whoever wanted to come was made welcome, and soon taken into the fold. Nobody looked round at the German when the Wilson Committee to Review the Financial Institutions held hearings about foreign competition in banking. Nobody asked for my nationality when I was appointed to the Royal Commission on the Legal Services. It is true that some keep on asking me about things German, only to find that having lived outside Germany since 1970 I know by now as much about things British. On the whole, Britain has made this alien feel very much at home.

The alien, moreover, came to learn about Britain. When the Royal Commission visited Northern Ireland, I admired the courage of the judges, and the apparent impartiality of members of the Bar Library and the Law Society; but I also concluded that the present state of affairs would not last. Too many people told me that their children had left and would not return. Too many also had personally experienced terrorism. There may not be a theoretical answer to the problem; but reality itself will give an answer, and I for one should be surprised if that answer was simply the status quo.

Once I visited my friend John Mackintosh (who, alas! died far too early), and spent a day with him in his constituency outside Edinburgh. This was the time of the devolution debate, and John was probably the Labour MP closest to the devolutionists. He believed in a federal Britain in which Scotland would play its part. Perhaps he dreamt of himself as the first Scottish Prime Minister. Coming from a federal country, I was naturally impressed. Indeed, I do not share the views of those who think that with the referendum of 1979 the question of devolution has gone away for good. At the same time, Britain has strangely managed to avoid a 'national question'. Most Continental countries have such national questions; many believe that their nation should include territories which are now outside their boundaries. Certainly, the German 'nation' was always larger than the country called Germany. Not so in Britain. The country admits happily to including several nations. There is the beautiful absurdity of 'home international' football games. Even the Irish nation, independent as it is in the country called Eire, is no practical worry. Irishmen can vote in Britain if they choose to, and election results in several constituencies in Merseyside, Clydeside, and elsewhere may well be determined by their vote. Thus, devolution may be an issue, but the nation is not. Felix Britannia!

An alien at the head of a British institution is naturally a bit of a curiosity. People wonder about him, express pleasure or suspicion, but above all they ask him what he thinks about them. Since I am very fond of the country, I have spoken up about it. Usually, I have praised or, if necessary, defended British institutions and attitudes. One of my newspaper articles, appropriately published by the *Financial Times*, was entitled 'Not by Bread Alone'. It sums up the essence of my defence: 'There is a fundamental liberty about life in Britain which is not easily found elsewhere.'[7] Whatever I said then in praise of Britain, stands. Indeed, I had once thought of putting it into a series of imaginary letters addressed to the country, which I should have published under the title, 'To Britain, with love'. But then the BBC asked me to help produce a series about the past, present and future of Britain. Clearly, this could not be a simple song of praise. There are problems, and it is by no means certain that Britain, with all its strengths, will be able to cope with them. To understand these problems is perhaps a useful beginning. It might even be that an alien who is both in and out, who does and does not belong, is well placed to help understand the British predicament.

This, then, is what I have to say in defence of trying to address those who have treated me so well, about their own affairs. Clearly, this book is not written by an impartial observer. It is not scholarship, not a dissertation, but a book of life, of personal ideas and feelings and observations, of arguments which may or may not be right, but which are intended to be helpful. This book shuns simple answers. There are in fact no patent medicines for social and economic ills. Yet there will be a hint or two about where the author would like to see the country go. Thus, this is a book of critical affection. It starts with Victorian Britain and its decline, and it ends with a look into the future which Britain shares with others; but throughout, it is concerned with the peculiar strengths which give this country its distinction.

A CENTURY OF DECLINE

Chapter Two
DECLINE WITHOUT FALL

Inevitably, the story of modern Britain begins with its economy. And the story of Britain's economy appears to be one of decline. Somehow, sometime, there emerged the first signs of that strange malady which has come to be called the 'British sickness' or 'British disease'.

Some say that the Great Exhibition of 1851 was the last expression of an unquestioned self-confidence of the new industrial Britain. The Crystal Palace itself seemed to embody the extraordinary progress of engineering skills and techniques. This was all the more true of the exhibits of industrial achievement from all over the world which were displayed in the Palace. For when it came to awarding medals for the most ingenious entries, most of them went to British inventors and engineers. 'Yet the generation of the Great Exhibition was to mark an end and not a beginning.' This, at any rate, is Martin Wiener's view, in his book on *English Culture and the Decline of the Industrial Spirit*.[1] Wiener quotes, as one of his witnesses, John Stuart Mill, who had said as early as 1850: 'I confess I am not charmed with the idea of life held out by those who think that the normal state of human beings is that of struggling to get on; that the trampling, crushing, elbowing, and treading on each other's heels, which form the existing type of social life, are the most desirable lot of human kind, or anything but the disagreeable symptoms of one of the phases of industrial progress.'[2]

A very English statement indeed! Such values will be examined more closely later, as will Wiener's interesting analysis. Yet John Stuart Mill's abhorrence of the industrial spirit is hardly proof of the decline of British industry in the 1850s. With the possible exception of America, there is no industrial country in which economic progress was not accompanied by the moans and groans of cultural pessimists; Germany, the country which was later to become the bugbear of

Britain's economy, had, if anything, more of the paradox of economic progress and cultural despair. There were slumps and booms after 1851; but the decades following the Great Exhibition were on the whole a period of considerable economic progress in Britain.

Progress, of course, is a human achievement which is not all sweetness and light. The confidence and enthusiasm of the Great Exhibition were one thing; but there was another side to them. Seven years before the Crystal Palace was completed, the young Karl Marx and his industrialist friend and fellow-author Frederick Engels, had met in the famous Manchester library, Chetham's, and studied the early political economists. For Marx, Manchester meant the first and, some would say, the only encounter with the slums of an industrial proletariat. Engels, one of whose father's factories was in Manchester, knew better. It was he who 'forsook the company and dinner parties, the port wine and champagne of the middle classes and devoted [his] leisure hours almost exclusively to intercourse with plain working men'.[3] The result was a book: *The Condition of the Working Class in England in 1844*, an early indictment of the social consequences of industrialisation. Later Marx was to add to this story, having read, at the British Museum, the reports of the Factory Inspectors and other material. He came to the conclusion that industrialisation creates an impoverished class which will, in due course, overturn capitalist society and build its own world. In this he was wrong. He also believed that the British experience would be repeated in every country which adopted industrial methods. Again he was wrong: there are almost as many stories of industrialisation as there are countries. But he and Engels and many others were certainly right to point out that the initial price of industrialisation was high. Alexis de Tocqueville, the observant traveller, put it in a nutshell when he described Manchester in his *Journeys to England and Ireland* of 1835: 'From this foul drain the greatest stream of human industry flows out to fertilize the whole world. From this filthy sewer pure gold flows. Here humanity attains its most complete development and its most brutish; here civilization works its miracles and civilized man is turned back almost into a savage.'[4]

Economic growth does not necessarily mean happiness – it is as well to bear this simple fact in mind. Measures of growth as economists use them are of necessity crude; they include things which most would regard as destructive, like the cost of car accidents, and they exclude important aspects of the quality of life. Thus, what we call 'gross national product (gnp)' or 'gross domestic product (gdp)' is but one indicator among others; but it is a useful indicator of economic progress. In terms of this indicator there was, throughout the 1880s and 1890s, but one country in the world which could compete with Britain: that was Australia; and Australia was a kind of Kuwait of the time, in that its wealth was largely based not on manufacturing, but on minerals and other primary products. Even in the mid-1890s, Britain clearly led the world's league table of economic achievement. But others were catching up. Today we know that whereas an average of sixteen other advanced countries showed, during the 'founders' period' of 1870–1913, an annual growth rate of 1.5, Britain remained at 1.0. Not surprisingly, therefore, Britain came to be overtaken by Germany, by the United States, later by other countries in Europe and elsewhere.

If one expresses the process in money terms, and extends it to the late 1970s, the differences between Britain and other countries are staggering:

League Tables of Countries
(annual income expressed in £'s sterling per capita)

1895		1977/8	
England & Wales	332	2765	UK
(Scotland)	262		
France	253	4425	France
USA	237	4830	USA
Germany	152	5210	W. Germany
Russia	61	1795	USSR
Japan	(25)	4240	Japan

By the end of the nineteenth century, per capita income in Britain was 332 pounds sterling. The next richest country (Australia apart) was France with 253 pounds. At the same time, per capita income in Germany was a mere 152 pounds, in Japan perhaps 25 pounds. Since then, income measured by the same standard has increased 170 times in Japan, 34 times in Germany, 17 times in France, but only 8 times in England. As a result, the United Kingdom today very nearly trails the league table of advanced countries; in any case, Britain finds itself in the relegation zone, always liable to drop to the second division.

Now, it is important not to be overawed by such figures. We have already seen that gross domestic product per capita and individual welfare, let alone personal happiness, are different things. Moreover, average figures tend to conceal a whole multitude of differences. At a time of overall decline, there may well be entire regions or industries which flourish. In any case, growth is but one measure of economic health. Not only individuals and societies, but economies can be perfectly sound without growing fast. Rapid growth, on the other hand, can be a straw fire – a goldrush or an oil glut for example.

The most important caveat concerning the interpretation of Britain's decline in growth is, however, a different one. League tables of economic performance are all very well, but what matters for people is their own condition of life. League tables apart, the plain fact is that per capita income in Britain has increased from some 320 pounds sterling in the 1890s to some 2800 pounds in the 1970s; in other words, it has multiplied almost nine times. There is no other period in history which has seen such enormous improvement. Indeed, this is not a story of decline; it is one of remarkable advance. However objectionable the statement may be to many, with its connotations of Harold Macmillan's Bedford speech of 1957, it is a matter of sober truth that most people in Britain have never had it so good.

What is often called the decline of Britain is therefore economic and relative. Economic decline need not mean social or political decline; though the three are obviously related in some ways. Relative decline, in a sense, need not mean decline at all. It simply means that others have done better than Britain, though Britain, too, has done well. What is more, Britain was the first country to do well, so that in a sense the people of Britain have reaped the benefits of industrialisation for longer, if not to a greater extent, than others.

Yet this is obviously not the whole story. Relative decline means, after all, that British industry lost its dynamics at a time during which others found it perfectly possible to move ahead. We are not talking about a world recession as all countries experience it in the early 1980s, but about a condition in which many countries made rapid economic progress, whereas Britain slowed down, if not to a standstill, then to halting, uncertain, almost reluctant, and in any case slow, motion. When did this happen? How did it happen? Why did it happen?

Explaining the 'British disease' has become a popular sport among scholars and journalists alike. Like all sports, it may be fun, but does not lead very far. However, a definition of the problem must be attempted, if only because it cannot be avoided.

There is first of all the question of when it all started. The notion that 1851 was the great watershed of Britain's industrial history has already been rejected. Progress continued long beyond that date, even if some of the early origins of decline can be discerned at the very heights of success. There is a great debate among economists and economic historians about whether real decline started in the 1880s or the 1890s. Certainly, the last two decades of the nineteenth century were a time in which people became aware of the fact that there were problems. The Commission on the Depression of Trade insisted in 1886 that 'if our position is to be maintained it must be by the exercise of the same energy, perseverance, self-restraint and readiness of resource by which it was originally created'.[6] Alfred Marshall noted that even earlier, by the 1870s, 'many of the sons of manufacturers' were 'content to follow mechanically the lead given by their fathers. They worked shorter hours; and they exerted themselves less to obtain new practical ideas.'[7] Certainly, the creation of Trafford Park in Manchester, Europe's first purpose-built industrial park, which was made possible by the Manchester Ship Canal, opened in 1894, was a deliberate effort designed to 'awaken England'. 'Wake up England, Trafford Park is awake!' was the slogan with which the new industrial estate, opened in 1902, was boosted in 1905. Yet it is hard to contradict those who argue that there was still a great deal of industrial strength in Britain right up to the First World War. The real watershed probably is the War.[8] After 1918, Britain never regained the confidence and strength which had marked its past throughout the nineteenth century, if not earlier.

Even if we leave to historians the debate over the date marking the beginning of the loss of Britain's industrial dynamism, one conclusion is clear: it did not start five, or twenty-five, or even forty years ago, but much earlier. The roots of Britain's contemporary problems reach deeply into its history, sixty years at least, if not a century.

How, then, did the great change come about which has led Britain from world leadership to the margin of the second division? The reasons will shortly become clear. However, in the first instance it is important to remember, when considering the economic history of Britain, the personal history of individuals. We have all known people who made good by learning and effort, who improved their position as well as their ways, and who then, slowly or sometimes suddenly, seemed to lose the ability to continue. In a sense, we all do. Every shining schoolboy ends up 'sans teeth, sans eyes, sans taste, sans everything'. But some stop earlier than others. Perhaps a spring has snapped inside them; perhaps they simply did not want to continue. Perhaps some great internal battle was going on between ambition and inertia, between wanting to grow and fearing change. We wonder what happened. Perhaps we mind, perhaps not. There are many tastes, and it is vain to dispute them. But it is a strange, and ultimately after all a depressing sight: a person who is growing and improving and then ceases to do so, stagnates, even reverts. The same can be true for a country.

Britain's economy, then, is a case of stunted growth. The enormous dynamism of its early decades first slowed down, then died away. Something strange happened, somewhere between 1870 and 1918, or more precisely, around the turn of the century. What was it?

Chapter Three
THE STRENGTHS OF WEAKNESS— THE WEAKNESSES OF STRENGTH

There are many ways of answering the question of why Britain fell behind. The first question to be considered is: what made Britain strong? Economies do not exist in a vacuum. They are anchored in people's values and social conditions. Nor is its economy all there is to a country. Britain may not have done as well as others economically, but in many other respects it has remained the envy of the world. In fact, Britain is known above all not for its weaknesses, but for its strengths. The British disease is of fairly recent origin, whereas the desire to emulate Britain's social and political institutions is an old one. *De te fabula narratur*, said Marx when he wrote of Britain: it is your story that is being told.[1] Marx was thinking of a gloomy story of poverty and revolution. Many others shared the view that Britain's story would be theirs; but they, by contrast, saw in Britain a 'future that works',[2] that is, a story of hope and of opportunity. For them, the strengths of Britain mattered more than its problems.

There are several ways of describing the strengths of Britain, but none that would not start with tradition itself, with *continuity*. Foreigners flock to England to look on at the manifestations of a tradition which they do not have. They often do not understand how real this tradition is. An American television company suggested to its British commentator on the Royal Wedding of 1981: 'And after the ceremony you have a quick interview with the Queen, and ask her how she liked the whole thing. . .' They thought the whole ceremony was a public relations exercise and not real. It is true that judges look distant in their wigs, and that the 'loyal toast' after dinner has become a permission to smoke rather than an expression of loyalty, and that 'naming' a person is a strange way for the Speaker of the House of

Commons to expel a member – but these and hundreds of other little symbols of tradition are nevertheless a unique characteristic of British life. They are not the somewhat artificial veneration of history, but the real presence of history today.

One day, some students of mine decided to stage a sit-in in our Registry in order to express their understandable dismay at cruel increases in the fees for overseas students. Since they would not leave voluntarily, I had to apply for a Court Order for possession. Before the Court, they argued that, as students, they had a right to be in the Registry. Ah! said the judge, but not at night. Why not? Because, the judge pointed out, there is an eighteenth-century precedent which says that the right to use a staircase does not imply the right to slide down the banister. The students laughed and left.

Such stories are not simply amusing. It is harder to change tradition than it is to change written laws. This means that in Britain the safeguards of liberty have been stronger than in many countries with written constitutions. No German who fled his country when the most liberal constitution in German history, that of Weimar, was suspended on Hitler's instigation by a simple Enabling Law feared that the absence of a written constitution would make Britain unsafe. Indeed, there is an example closer to home. During the inter-war years, the bacillus of fascism infected the world. It conquered the body politic in Italy and Spain, Austria and Germany. It came close to doing so in France. But in Britain, the former Socialist, Oswald Mosley, and his Blackshirts, remained an episode; there was never a question of their taking over the country. Is it too far-fetched to suggest that the strength of tradition proved a more effective safeguard than the constitutions, laws and courts elsewhere?

Continuity, then, is one of the strengths of Britain; another is *excellence*. To the present day, no country has more Nobel Prize winners per head than Britain. Nor is that the only sign of excellence. At the advanced end of technology, Britain has always excelled. There is, as it were, a straight line from Hargreave's Spinning Jenny and Stephenson's Rocket to the early computers and to Concorde (though one is bound to admit that this line is sloping downwards so far as industrial application is concerned).

There are other expressions of excellence. Britain's universities are the envy of the world. They provide the best academic education at minimum cost. Whereas on the European continent, students usually require five or six years in expensive institutions and unstructured courses to get a degree, and half of them drop out in the process, the average English degree course still takes three years, involves personal tutoring, and less than fifteen per cent drop out. Incidentally, research, too, is both cheaper and more distinguished in Britain than elsewhere in Europe; the number of Nobel Prize winners is not the only index.

The word 'elite' has come to be tabu in Britain as elsewhere. An egalitarian age does not like the idea that some are better than others. Or rather, it does not like to admit the fact. In one sense, this is understandable. No human being should derive any special rights or privileges from particular, perhaps unique, qualities. But the basic equality of rank which all citizens share cannot detract from their many inequalities as human beings, and indeed from the fact that some are first-rate playwrights, geneticists, administrators, film producers, stockbrokers, barristers. The outstanding quality of such categories of persons is, in Britain, matched by that of institutions, of which some have become words of praise, and of emulation all over the world: 'the City', 'Harley Street', *The Times*, 'the BBC', 'Oxford', and, of course, 'LSE' are but some examples out of many.

These examples have something in common quite apart from their excellence: one might call it autonomy or, with a precise use of the word, *liberty*. Britain may not have kept a market economy for very long; but the country has certainly maintained its market society. By market is meant the free interplay of autonomous and decentralised units for the welfare of the whole. In economic affairs, the state on the one hand, and overly big companies on the other have long robbed this interplay of its freedom; in social organisation, it has continued to the present day. To understand this point better, it may be useful to think back to the medieval battles between the barons and the king. In most European countries, the King won sooner or later. This was notably true in France, but of course was the case in Russia, in Austria, in Italy too. In Germany – well, in Germany it took a long time before one Emperor won the day in 1871, but the men who ruled before were not barons of a kingdom; they were little and not-so-little kings of their own. In other words, there was no Germany, there was just a collection of kingdoms and principalities. Not so in Britain. Britain was undoubtedly a kingdom. But the rights of the king remained circumscribed, even before a Parliament arose to check them. Barons and king had established a precarious relationship of delimited rights.

In important respects, the barons remained autonomous, although in others, they granted the king his rights.

This excursion into (somewhat simplified) history is useful in order to understand a whole set of British institutions and attitudes. Take the BBC. It is publicly financed, like radio and television in Continental countries, and could therefore be expected to be run by government appointees (as in France), or by councils on which the political parties are represented (as in Germany). Yet it is not. While the Director General is appointed by the Governors of the Corporation, to whom he is accountable, the twelve Governors are independent personalities appointed by the Queen in Council for a fixed term. They do not represent interest groups. Their independence is assumed, and by and large they act in accordance with this assumption.

Or take the professions. In a significant sense they have public functions. After all, the law originates in Parliament and applies to all. It could therefore be argued that the legal profession should be controlled by government. There should be a public system of legal education, state examinations, admission to the profession through government auspices, control of professional ethics by government. All this is in fact the case on the Continent. In Britain, however, the professions have retained an independent status. They themselves organise legal education, admission to the profession, and the maintenance of standards. They are, as it were, one of the institutional barons of a society which has never become a state society.

There are other examples. The City is largely self-governing, with the Bank of England playing the role of referee. The Bank itself was, characteristically, privately controlled until 1946. Universities are almost entirely publicly financed; yet government allocation of funds is organised through a University Grants Committee on which there are more academics than administrators. The Civil Service is independent, non-political, in a sense which has come to be unknown in most other countries. The same Secretary of the Cabinet may serve two or three different Prime Ministers and he will do so fairly, competently, and without ever bringing his personal political views to bear on decisions. Indeed, after a while, he may cease to have such views. Independence in the British sense is a remarkable virtue.

Calling such independence liberty is perhaps slightly misleading. By liberty we usually understand such things as the freedom of speech and of political choice, freedom from arbitrary arrest, and the like. It could be argued, however, that the most effective institutional guarantee of liberty is the autonomy of institutions, that is, the absence of the State with a capital S from the lives of individuals in as many fields as possible. The opposite, the universal presence of the State, is certainly oppressive. The State societies of the European Continent are always capable of tightening the reins; indeed, the reins are tight enough at the best of times. Wherever one goes, the State is there already. One needs identity papers if one goes for a walk; an official registration if one rents a flat; a stamped metal mark if one has a dog, to say nothing of state diplomas of many kinds; and above all, stamps, stamps, stamps. Where in England a man's or a woman's word is sufficient, a Continental always needs an official stamp.

Lest the notion be misunderstood, such liberty is of course not confined to institutions. It is reflected in people's behaviour. Traditionally, people in Britain do not wait for the State to come to their aid. There is a remarkable history of self-help. Voluntary organisations have always blossomed; and even today, it is more usual to rely on voluntary action than to ask government to step in. The most dramatic example of this attitude is the 'black economy'. It is the one branch of British economic life which is not affected by decline. Figures are hard to come by, but it would not be surprising if some ten per cent of the gross domestic product of Britain was produced in the 'black economy', and a much larger percentage of people are engaged in one way or another in work, the payment for which is not taxed. It would perhaps be cynical to say that the 'black economy' makes unemployment bearable; more often than not those who do 'black' work are in fact employed, frequently in the public service, notably in local government. But the point is that the 'black economy' shows, in Britain as in Italy, that there is a sense of initiative, however hard regulations and controls try to quench it. It is ultimately not true that the economy is left out of the market society of Britain; or rather, this is true for the official economy only. The unofficial economy is Britain's version of the market economy, and of economic liberty. One must hope that no-one will try to destroy it out of misplaced Puritanism or a belief in the benevolent state.

There is a fourth strength of British society which is perhaps the most important of all. It has to do with people's attitudes, with the way they behave to each other, and also with the quotation from John Stuart Mill in an earlier chapter. There, Mill deplored 'the existing type of social life', which, he said, consisted of 'the trampling, crushing, elbowing and treading on each other's heels'. Such behaviour undoubtedly exists, even in Britain; but it is certainly not how an alien sees the country. On the contrary, it is on the Continent as well as across the Atlantic that the great rat-race dominates people's lives. There, individuals are all set to compete with each other. Britain, on the other hand, is not a society of individual competition, it is a society of *solidarity*.

For some, the notion of solidarity may evoke the concept of the 'spirit of Dunkirk', or pictures of women beavering away in ammunition factories or filling sandbags while their men fight for their freedom: that is to say, the solidarity of the country as a whole. This, however, is not what is meant. Solidarity can in fact be divisive for the country as a whole, however inclusive it is for the individual. There is the solidarity of classes, for example. Equally importantly, there is the solidarity of smaller occupational groups, of skill groups; so many 'demarcation' disputes between trade unions have to do with where people belong, that is, with the boundary of the unit within which the rules of solidarity hold. There can be the temporary solidarity of, say, football fans, or even rioters; and there is the more lasting solidarity of pubs and clubs, places and, unfortunately, races.

The point to be emphasised is that in Britain most people belong in one way or another. They are a part of some group which, and with which, they can identify. They know that belonging means being a good chum, pal, fellow. So they are nice to their peers. They actually try not to stand out from them, but to be like them. They help out and get on and cover up, whatever the need may be. The attitude can be extended to others. Larry and Tim and John and Cato took me into their group in the general ward of Amersham General Hospital. Indeed, the essential kindness and even non-violence which used to be one of the most notable characteristics of British life, has its origin in this pervasive sense of solidarity. One obviously did not fight one's peers; and since one knew where one belonged, one did not have to fight others.

This also explains the happiness of the British, so much commented upon. Who knows what exactly happiness is, especially if Gallup pollsters ask a random sample of people whether or not they are happy?[3] But when they do, Britain regularly comes out on top, or close to the top. On the whole, the British probably are happier than others. 'Stress' may be an English word, but it is, if anything, a Continental and American phenomenon. There are three times as many suicides in

Germany as there are in England. Is it unfair to suspect that this has something to do with the fact that most people in Britain are supported by a network of their peers? There are seven times as many murders in New York as in London. Is it wrong to assume that even in the jungle of inner cities the young have a greater sense of belonging in Britain than elsewhere?

This book is not, or at any rate not only, a eulogy of Britain. It is time, therefore, to stop the praise of Britain's strengths, and take a more sober look at them, as well as at the changes which they have undergone. Continuity, excellence, liberty, solidarity are an acceptable collection of virtues, at least for most; but for every virtue there is a vice, and many are more impressed by the vices, the weaknesses which go with the strengths, than by the virtues.

To begin with solidarity. That rat-race which characterizes, say, Germany and America has of course its causes and its effects. They are, among others, economic. Certainly, an attitude of individual competition is more likely to help increase productivity than one of solidarity. Individual competition means that everybody is trying to do as well, and to make as much, as he possibly can; collective solidarity means that people try to get on with others, and tend to be satisfied with what they have got. It may well be that the prevalence of the values of solidarity is one of the reasons why the productivity of British industry has lagged behind. After all, there is a world of difference between tea breaks and productivity bonuses. Thus, the very virtues which make it so pleasant to live in Britain may also account for its economic weakness – and the reverse is true elsewhere: the very opportunities for economic success which characterise American society make the life of the rat-race so strenuous.

There is another point about solidarity which it is worth making here. Karl Marx, in his analysis of class conflict and revolution, had little time for the values of individual competition. He argued that the competition between individuals destroys class solidarity. Decades later, in 1907, Marx's countryman Werner Sombart observed, in his essay on *Why Is There No Socialism in the United States?*,[4] that individual opportunity and mobility make collective social and political action unlikely in America. What does this mean for Britain? Is Britain the one country in which Marx's gloomy predictions of class warfare and revolution could come true?

But let us return to the weaknesses of Britain's strengths. The autonomy of institutions may mean liberty, but it can also mean the absence of any central purpose. Autonomous institutions would not have brought about the striking economic successes of Japan; on the contrary, the characteristic feature of Japanese institutions is that they are all linked, in highly effective ways which escape the foreigner's eye. In Germany, it was less the linkage of all institutions than their domination by a few, notably the state and the banks, which helped the economic process along. A similar case could be made for France. In Britain, on the other hand, everyone went his own way – with the exception, paradoxically, of the nationalised industries. For some strange reason, the virtues of institutional autonomy stopped short of the area in which they are most needed. Heads of nationalised industries get ministerial instructions much of the time, and have to appear before parliamentary committees far more often than is good for their business. Thus, autonomy did not help the official economy; and however much one may praise the 'black economy', in the end its very existence documents a failure of the system.

Then, excellence. It has already been hinted that magnificent inventions do not translate themselves into industrial practice. Indeed, it is perfectly possible to have a flourishing industry without being very inventive. By now, Japan has caught up in research and development as well; but many still remember Japanese industrial 'spies' travelling about Europe with their cameras in order to find the models to follow. Prime Minister Heath hoped that Britain's membership of the European Community would lead to a happy marriage between Britain's inventions and high technology, and the Continent's management skills. But this is not the way things happen. In the end, Britain got stuck with its extremes of achievement, and at best translated them into Concordes and Rolls Royces, not Caravelles and Volkswagens.

It is in this context that tradition, and continuity too, reveal their weakness. A modern industrial economy needs change. It needs individuals to be adaptable, prepared, for instance, to move house and settle in another part of the country, that is to say, to break with cherished ties. It also needs adaptability in industry. No one notion is more important in the contemporary industrial world than that of adjustment. Unless advanced economies adjust, they will fall behind forever. Both adjustment and individual adaptability are, however, not made easier by a strong sense of continuity in individuals and institutions, and by the dominance of tradition. It appears that Britain has got stuck with its wonderful virtues, that these very virtues have prevented it from moving ahead.

If there is any truth to this analysis, it suggests two items for the interim balance of this story. First, it could be argued that it was the very strengths of British society which prevented the progress of Britain's economy beyond a certain point. Britain's stunted growth is due to a simple fact: the new developments of industry stretched the social strengths of the country almost to breaking point, but then these strengths prevailed. Continuity, excellence, autonomy and solidarity were too strong to be destroyed by the demands of a modern industrial economy. Faced with the choice, the country settled for its familiar strengths, and thereby prevented the progress of its economy. Britain's economic weakness is merely the other side of its social strength.

But this is only the first of the preliminary conclusions. Perhaps every country has to pay the price for its strengths; perhaps every strength is compensated for by a weakness somewhere. But in Britain, a rather agreeable balance was achieved. By 1913, and indeed beyond, Britain had attained a satisfactory level of economic development, while at the same time maintaining some of the strengths of its society which date back far beyond the Industrial Revolution. Britain had, in other words, produced a peculiar and quite pleasing equilibrium. People began to benefit from the new-found wealth of industrialism, but they did not see their whole lives dominated by industrial values. John Stuart Mill's nightmare did not come true. On the contrary, the industrial classes, whether management or labour, absorbed the pre-industrial values of their country. There was, to be sure, deprivation. There was also violence, visible and invisible. Yet there is a sense in which it could be argued that in Britain, the industrial classes created a balance of success and happiness which few if any others ever found. This was Britain, the happy industrial society.

Chapter Four
DECLINE AND (ALMOST) FALL

This *was* Britain, the happy industrial society. At the very least, the past tense of this statement must be emphasised to put it in proper perspective. For one thing, an equilibrium like the one described never really exists. There were many who left the country throughout the decades; and they obviously emigrated because they were unhappy with life in Britain. There were others who did very badly indeed; the new industrial wealth was shared in highly uneven ways. There were those who fell through the net of solidarity; indeed Britain was a very restless country despite its basic social cohesion. But above all, the equilibrium did not last. Perhaps it was too good to last; perhaps no equilibrium ever lasts. In any case, the decades since 1918 are decades of decline. What is more, this time the decline affected both sides of the balance, the economic and the social.

To begin with the economic side. The inter-war period was one of mixed fortunes for all advanced countries. Even so, Britain did worse than the average of the others. On balance, Britain's growth rates were somewhat lower, unemployment was exceedingly high, and it took the country a very long time to get over the Great Depression. Then, after the Second World War, came the great world boom. It had, as Walt Rostow has shown in his *World Economy* (if one did not know it already) no rival in economic history.[1] Never before has there been as dramatic an economic upswing as in the quarter-century following 1948 (or, for some countries, 1945; for the United States, 1940). Yet Britain all but missed the economic miracle of the 1950s and 1960s. This is an overstatement; compared with its own past Britain did rather well in this period; yet it was during these twenty-five years that Britain finally dropped to the relegation zone of the world's top economic league table.

Then, from 1960 onwards, Britain's economic decline took on a new dimension. Since that time, short periods of boom apart, Britain began to decline not only relatively but absolutely. Nor do we have to rely on gross domestic product (gdp) figures to make this point. To use Samuel Brittan's words: 'Since 1960, however, an absolute gap [between the United Kingdom and the main European countries] has emerged – whether measured by output, or real wages, or whether the comparisons are made at market or purchasing parity exchange rates, or by the fallible impressions of personal travel.'[2] In more recent years, the situation has been compounded by the fact that Britain scored badly with respect to both inflation and unemployment.

Thus today Britain has an economy which finds it difficult to achieve even zero growth, an inflation rate in double figures, an unemployment figure of three million or more, and real wages which have fallen far behind those of all comparable countries. Actually, in terms of textbooks of economics, it could be argued that Britain's real wages are still too high. They have grown faster – in certain fluke years, much faster – than productivity, so that it can still be said of most of those in work that they have never had it so good. Even so, they do not have it anywhere near as good as their peers on the Continent or in North America. What is more, since there is no sign of a general economic upswing for the country, things can only get worse. This is real economic decline.

Moreover, at this time, economic decline is accompanied by serious threats to every one of the sources of social strengths already listed. This is most obvious with respect to the values subsumed under the notion of solidarity. Is it still pleasant to live in Britain? Are people still kind? Is the country still non-violent? At a time at which there is rioting in the streets, looting of shops, at which the crime rate rises rapidly and many young people have never known a peer group worth belonging to (unless it were one of skinheads, or punks), the old notions of sweetness and light seem ironical rather than real. There are other indices of change. It is true that Britons have always sought success on distant shores – if not gold at Klondike, then a good job in Canada, or in Germany, or in Saudi-Arabia; but today the migration balance, especially of 'professional' and 'managerial' people, is significantly negative. Some fifty thousand skilled people leave the country each year, and while the majority return at a later date, many stay away for good. Not surprisingly, suicide rates are also rising. The net of solidarity no longer supports everybody; there is a growing sense of anomie, of lawlessness and isolation.

The reasons for such changes are many. No doubt, travelling and television, and the comparisons which they suggest, have played their part. Also, continuing economic decline, especially when it turns from relative to absolute decline, has taken its toll. Even at the best of times, inner cities are hardly a showcase for values of kindness and belonging.

But no such list of changes can ignore the most important of all, which is not the emigration of skilled Britons abroad, but the immigration of unskilled West Indians and Asians by the million. The fact that today nearly five per cent of all Britons are coloured, marks the most significant single social change in the country for decades. For British society has not been able to cope with immigration from the so-called 'new Commonwealth'. The middle classes have ignored their new countrymen; and the working classes have pushed them aside, rejected them. As Indians and Pakistanis begin to succeed in small business, especially in the service sector, resentment against them grows among the unemployed. The first battles between skinheads and young Asians tell the story. In any case, the cultural difference of brown Asians is for many as hard to take as the allegedly different work habits of black West Indians. The new immigrants remain, even if they succeed economically, a painful reminder of national failure rather than a part of a society once so proud of its inclusive sense of oneness and solidarity.

This was not necessary. To anticipate 'rivers of blood' as a result of immigration was a very un-British thing to do. It is true that it is easier to extend the arms of solidarity to those of similar appearance and culture. Homogeneity helps to bring about non-violence and kindness. But it is not a necessary condition. Indeed, Peregrine Worsthorne was surely right, when he pointed out in a courageous article in the *Sunday Telegraph* ('The Right way to cure our racial ills'[3]) that it would have been in the best Conservative tradition of Britain to welcome the new citizens and turn them into true Britons, even into nationalists proud of their country. 'Unless the newcomers are taught to be proud of their new homeland, expressly indoctrinated in its culture and history, the process of acclimatisation is bound to take many generations to complete.' However, so far such advice has not been followed. Instead, along with other factors, the multiracial character of British society has led to the denting, if not to the crumbling, of one of the great strengths of the country, its social values. It may not be too late to turn the tide;

but it would be overly optimistic to claim that there are any signs of this.

Then there is the liberty, the autonomy of institutions. This has been under pressure for many years; and while so far most of the institutions in question have resisted such pressure, it is permissible to wonder how long this can last. In the case of universities, the erosion of autonomy, and of the position of the University Grants Committee, is due to the crisis of public expenditure. The apparent need for cuts, the extent of which is usually discovered at the last minute, has resulted in the disappearance of the 'quinquennial system' by which universities received grant promises for a period of five years at a time. Instead, they now receive one-year grants, and even these too late to make autonomous planning possible. When it became clear that these grants would be reduced in real terms, autonomy was further eroded; the University Grants Committee had to act as an agent of government and decide who gets more and who gets less.

If pressures in the case of universities are primarily financial, they are social and political in other instances. The Royal Commission on the Legal Services was set up because it was felt that lawyers were making too much money without proper control. Some may even have hoped that a National Legal Service would be created alongside the National Health Service. The Committee to Review the Functioning of Financial Institutions was not only concerned with the question of why the world's greatest financial centre has failed to supply the funds for investment in British industry, but also with that of control, the role of the Bank, necessary rules and sanctions. Both aspects of its work led some to demand greater accountability to, if not intervention by, public institutions.

Such examples could be multiplied. What they show is a growing distrust of autonomous institutions, and a widespread demand for an accountability which in fact means state control. Rather than a movement to liberate nationalised industries from the fetters of government intervention, there is pressure for the nationalisation of other institutions. This is true also with respect to the third strength of British life, excellence. One of the least plausible objections to the differential approach chosen by the University Grants Committee in its allocation of cuts is that such an approach creates a three-tier system of universities. What is wrong with having some places which are truly first-rate? One of the least plausible objections to the separation of the legal profession into barristers and solicitors is that some of the best minds are creamed off to the bar. What is wrong with having a judiciary, and a trial system, of the highest quality? Yet such objections are widespread, and it has become increasingly difficult to counter them.

The most difficult issue in this context is, of course, that of independent schools ('public' schools). It would clearly be wrong to identify independence and excellence; some private schools are second-rate in every respect. But some are not; and from all accounts it seems that public schools attract a disproportionate number of the most gifted children of the country, especially since the abolition of grammar schools. This may well be regrettable. In theory, Shirley Williams is probably right that one of the causes of what is often called the system of class division in Britain is the division in education between independent and state schools.[4] But if a hundred years ago Britain had introduced a state system for all – as Germany and France had done even earlier – the necessary differentiation would have occurred within the state system. After all, the German *Gymnasium*, and France's *grandes écoles*, while public institutions, are not exactly egalitarian. But destroying differentiation today will probably mean destroying opportunities for excellence. This is a controversial subject, and it would be wrong to be too dogmatic about it. Yet experience shows that it is very difficult indeed to create differentiation by deliberate action. Once an existing system of differentiation is destroyed, it will be replaced, for some considerable time, by one of grey similarity, not to say equality. While it is arguable that it might have been better for the country if it had created one school system for all, one cannot re-write history. To create such a system today is to invite the destruction of opportunities for excellence.

All the points mentioned in this chapter lead back, of course, to the first strength of Britain, tradition and continuity. Every one of the trends and arguments mentioned indicates discontinuities, breaks with tradition. This is appropriate, for tradition has come to be widely under attack in Britain. There are complaints about the expenditure of the Royal Family, and they do not come only from Mr Willie Hamilton, MP; there are criticisms of the detachment of judges in their wigs, or of the irrelevance of ceremonial occasions in many institutions. Interest in ceremony is probably greater in most other countries of the world than it is in Britain.

But above all, there are strong and public demands for discontinuity. Indeed, if one looks at Britain today, one must come to the conclusion that discontinuity rather than continuity is the order of the day. Both traditional political parties advocate discontinuity; and the third, the Liberal-Social Democratic Alliance, documents discontinuity by its very existence. Twice in the 1970s, in 1970 and in 1979, Conservative governments have been elected on a platform of discontinuity. Both Mr Heath and Mrs Thatcher wanted to turn Britain into a kind of Germany; or, to put it less polemically, they wanted to transform a solidarity society into one of individual competition. Their main objective was in fact a change in social attitudes, so that Britain, like other industrial countries, would learn to concentrate on increasing productivity and making economic growth real. If both failed, this is a testimony to the strength of the sense of continuity in Britain; but that they tried, and won a majority for doing so, surely documents a widespread desire to explore new and different ways.

The Labour Party too has increasingly come to advocate a fundamental break with Britain's past. Whereas Prime Minister Callaghan governed in the Disraeli tradition of 'one nation', the next generation of Labour leaders wants to turn the institutions of the country upside down. Their main interest is not in economic growth, of course, but in social justice. Thus excellence for them means privilege, and autonomy the exploitation of special status. Both have to be done away with in the interests of justice. Labour too, in demanding such changes, follows models which are not traditionally British.

All this may not be so true of Liberals and Social Democrats. But the general fact remains that tradition and continuity are hardly the dominant forces in Britain today. Now, neither this nor the other points made in this chapter must be overstated. Traces of Britain's strengths can still be found in its contemporary reality. There are still people who come to Britain because of these strengths. In any case, it would be cowardly and defeatist to sink into a mood of gloom and doom. If anything, there is too much of it in contemporary Britain. 'We in Britain are a confused and unhappy people,' says Peter Jay.[5] He is probably exaggerating. Even so, confusion and unhappiness there are. This book is intended to reduce rather than increase them. It is not a gloom and doom book.

It is true that Britain's economy has declined to a point at which people's welfare is at risk. It is also true that the great strengths of the country are under threat. This means that change will have to take place, like it or not. In fact, it is taking place already. But in order to know where this change should lead, it is essential first to be clear about what if anything is wrong with people's attitudes and the country's institutions. One has to discover also why Britain finds it so difficult to define its identity in the world. This is what the following three parts of this book are about. Once the story of the gloomy, as well as the brighter realities of Britain has been completed, perhaps one or two paths can be traced into a future which is more than an empty promise and offers greater life chances to more people.

CLASS, AND OTHER ATTITUDES

Chapter Five
THE VANISHING OF THE INDUSTRIAL SPIRIT

Economists, not unnaturally, prefer economic explanations of economic facts. Yet in the case of Britain, such explanations strangely fail. Was economic growth held back by cyclical fluctuations caused by stop-go financial policies? In fact, the relation between economic cycles and growth is less dramatic in Britain than elsewhere. Was low investment the reason? In the relevant periods, investment in Britain was at least as high as in other countries. Did Britain suffer from unfavourable terms of trade? Balance-of-payments constraints were clearly not the dominant reason for Britain's weak export performance. Is government spending too high? It is no higher than in more successful countries. Does high taxation discourage people? Britain stands somewhere in the middle of the world league table of overall taxation. Samuel Brittan, who dismisses such theories one by one, then turns to trade unions, and the class system.[1] Peter Mathias concludes similarly that Britain's problem 'cannot be explained just in simple terms of economic hypotheses such as wage rates, shifting terms of trade or deteriorating natural resources'. Martin Wiener quotes Peter Mathias to prove his own point that 'the question of the causes of British economic decline remains beyond the sole grasp of economists'.[2] These causes are, to quote Peter Jay, 'deep-seated and general, embedded in the very organization of our society'.[3] They have to do, in other words, not with tangible economic factors, but with people's attitudes, and with the institutions which shape these attitudes'.

Martin Wiener's analysis has been, perhaps a little unfairly, dismissed in an earlier chapter. He probably is wrong in arguing that 1851 marks the beginning of Britain's decline. But this does not detract from the value of his central thesis, which is that Britain either never was, or soon ceased to be, a genuinely industrial society. As Dean Inge of St. Paul's put it concisely and clearly at the time of the Great Depression: 'The whole episode which made England the workshop of the world was alien to the spirit and character of the English people.'⁴ There are many ways of documenting this point. One is the striking emphasis on the value of rural living and the desirability of its slower pace, in British literature as well as politics. For the English, of whom a higher percentage lives in cities than that of most other peoples, 'England' is a green country, a country of grass and trees and quaint old villages, not of chimneys and railways and high-rise concrete monsters; this, at any rate, is how people like to see their habitat. There may be differences between the North and the South in this respect as in others; but ultimately, the South has prevailed. Its pre-industrial, or rather non-industrial, values have come to dominate the consciousness of all.

Sometimes, the two worlds, the green world of rural England and the black world of industry, meet in a physical way. The Vale of Belvoir in Leicestershire is the epitome of the English dream: rolling green country with pastures and fields, all dominated by the castle of the Dukes of Rutland. But underneath all this, coal has been found. So the battle between past and present is joined. It looks as if the battle is going to end as a draw, which means that in an important sense the countryside will prevail.

Rural images evoke rural people and their attitudes. In an urban society, there are not many of them left. Indeed, the great exodus from the country in the 18th and 19th centuries did at first create a new industrial class. There will be more to say about that later. But strangely, as this class grew older, or perhaps as its children looked at the toil and grime of their parents' lives, they remembered what seemed to them better days. Increasingly, they came to regard the rural gentry, or some bowdlerised version of it, as their model. The sons of industrialists were either 'gentrified' or they remained outsiders; sometimes even the fathers managed the transition. Throughout the Victorian period of hard work, and of ascetic discipline, the 'gentlemanly' ideal of the 'educated amateur' remained the dominant model. The gentleman, of course, does not exert himself too much. In any case, he does not spend his life striving and struggling and forgoing all immediate pleasures. Material improvement is not his prime interest, much as he likes the comforts of life. Nor is this liking for a slower and more enjoyable life than industry can provide confined to those who have succeeded. Some early socialist theorists denounced as fiercely as the spokesmen of the upper classes the 'gospel of whatever we've got, to get more' as well as that of 'wherever we are, to go somewhere else'.[5] This was Ruskin; and Tawney added his comment for good measure: 'That obsession with economic issues is as local and transitory as it is repulsive and disturbing.'[6] What Tawney disliked above all about work in the new industrial society was that the worker had to work for a wage and could no longer choose, as he had been able to do in earlier centuries, to 'work on the land as a squatter'.[7] Could it be that Eric Hobsbawm is wrong after all when he describes as a 'pretence' the notion that 'the Englishman is a thatched-cottager or country squire at heart'?[8] Ruskin and Tawney and many others were of course arguing against the new industrial class of Victorian times; but their socialism strangely resembled the older values of a class which had managed to survive the Industrial Revolution.

The drift of such observations is clear: while England invented the Industrial Revolution, it never liked its consequences. For a brief period, a generation or at most two, it looked as if Samuel Smiles and his bestseller *Self-Help*, which sold 130,000 copies in the thirty years following its first publication in 1859, was going to prevail. But he did not. Very soon, the English found ways and means of escaping from the values and attitudes that went with the new industrial world. They did in fact escape, at least in their minds. Somehow, they managed to preserve the memory of an earlier world. Where this did not work, as in the case of the new middle class swept to prominence by the Industrial Revolution, the readers of Samuel Smiles as it were, they blended old and new in remarkable ways. As a result, attitudes soon became neither 'pre-industrial' nor 'post-industrial', but non-industrial. The 'episode' of industrialisation all but disappeared from memory. Today, Britain is that strange paradox, a non-industrial industrial society.

An idea of such importance should be explored. Pursuing this idea in three different directions, may advance the story as it unfolds. There is first of all people's attitude to work. Tawney's regret that there is no alternative left to wage labour leads him to the conclusion that liberty will now have to be secured 'within the industrial system'.[9] Since escape is impossible, industrial work itself has to be made free, that is, autonomous and meaningful. This is a tall order, and it would be wrong to claim that anything of the kind has in fact happened in Britain. If it has happened at all, others, like the Swedes, have tried harder to achieve this end. Yet there is something about British attitudes to work which in a roundabout way achieves the same objective.

At first sight, there is a strange paradox about work in Britain. On the one hand, it consumes a greater part of people's lives than in most comparable countries; on the other hand, people seem to work much less hard than elsewhere. Work for most is still the centre of their lives. If ever there was a work society, it is Britain. One is not surprised to learn, from a comparative study by European trade unions, that the average Briton worked, in 1980, 238 hours more than the average Continental European. 238 hours – that is almost six weeks, for most! Paid holidays are shorter than elsewhere; there are fewer public holidays; and the institution of the 'bridge' between a public holiday and the nearest Saturday or Sunday is not yet general; indeed, conditions of work are generally less favourable to the modern industrial employee in Britain than they are in the rest of Europe. But then, the British are perhaps not modern industrial employees.

The importance of work is not confined to quantified facts. It is a matter of attitudes, too. This is the reason, of course, why unemployment is felt to be as much of a curse as is, say, inflation in Germany, or social exclusion in Japan. When Prince Philip, perhaps in a slightly unguarded moment, said in an interview that he did not understand why people on the one hand wanted more leisure, and on the other hand complained about unemployment, he made a valid, but also a rather un-British point. Of course, trade unions talk about shorter working hours; but the British do not necessarily want more leisure, however much they like their races and fishing and the rest. They are quite happy to spend the major part of their waking hours on their jobs. The notion of office workers starting at 7.30 in the morning, and going home at 3.30 or 4 o'clock in the afternoon, or factory workers starting at 6.30 and going home at 2.30 or 3 o'clock, in order to do other things, is by no means as general as it is on the Continent or in the United States. For one thing, many people do not like to start work at 7.30, let alone at 6.30 in the morning. Leisure still means evenings, weekends, holidays; it is a small and separate part of everyday life.

The other side of this picture is that one lives at work, that is to say, one does not go to work in order to work, but in order to spend an agreeable day. This is an overstatement, of course, but worth pursuing for a moment. There are local councils which have so-called Works Departments, the only function of which seems to be to keep people on the payroll. If they are sent to do something, it is pathetic to watch them. Council workers are highly visible, though hardly typical. Yet there are other cases in point. Tea breaks, for example, are a British invention. And here as elsewhere, the classes meet in a peculiar fashion. The equivalent of the tea break with directors or professional people is drinks before lunch; the advantage they have over tea-drinking workers is that the drinks are in fact followed by a luncheon as well. Whereas working people stretch their work so that it begins to look like leisure, managers and professional people constrain their leisure so that it has at least the appearance of work.

Overstatements apart, any foreigner who watches the British at work cannot help being amazed at their leisurely pace. In this, the division of labour helps; few people would dream of helping out if something has broken down. Instead, one waits for the 'experts' to turn up. Indeed, it would be interesting to know how much time working people in Britain spend waiting for something. This, incidentally, is not said with any critical intention. What we are describing is one of the reasons for the very pleasantness of life in Britain which is so widely, and so rightly admired. It is not, of course, a prescription for high productivity. But then, productivity! Again, it is instructive to cite the socialist, R. H. Tawney, who said in 1920: 'When the Press clamours that the one thing needed to make this island an Arcadia is productivity, and more productivity, and yet more productivity, that is . . . the confusion of means with ends.'[10] In other words, work is about life, not life about work. Britain's version of liberty is living at work rather than just living for work – and this may well be a more plausible liberty than that of the Continental who works his guts out on some other job when he has left his job, and who never stops working.

This leads to a second, more familiar, point which has to do with education and with the kinds of jobs preferred by people who have enjoyed a higher education. The point is familiar, because many have accused Britain's educational system of failing to instil the industrial spirit in its pupils and students. The accusation is misguided. The notion that schools and colleges can change the world around them is an illusion both of the right and the left: the right thinks that universities are subversive; and the left tries to subvert at least the Labour Party with the help of teachers and lecturers. In fact, educational institutions are much more likely to reflect the world around them. If graduates do not go into industry, the reason is that industry does not pay as well as the professions, or even government, and that the life it offers is less agreeable. People go for money and status and other pleasures which jobs can offer; and no attempt by schools and colleges to discourage them from doing so promises any success at all.

It is therefore not by way of accusation, but in an effort to understand, that the preferred choices of young people, and the style of their education, should be noted. The professions, the financial institutions, the media and government are clearly preferred vocational choices of the most gifted among the young. Industry is, at best, a second, if not a third choice. The result is that Britain's economy is strong in the service sector. Indeed, sometimes people need to be reminded that this sector is a part of the economy, and is actually making money, even if this consists of 'invisible earnings', in the terminology of trade. Such strength is in some ways surprising, because educational institutions still prefer the 'educated amateur'. However, the 'amateur' is educated by having a considerable part of his professional training on the job, as an articled clerk, a pupil, a research assistant, a trainee acountant, and the like. An almost medieval combination of academic training in generalities and practical training in specifics has been maintained. How different this is from the path which leads to the German *Diplomingenieur*, let alone the French graduate of the *École Nationale d'Administration* (ENA)!

Somewhere behind all this there is what might be called the missing industrial centre. By this is not meant a geographical centre, or one of particular branches of industry, but a social centre, a core of values which radiates throughout society. The fact that it has been missing in Britain for some time, is all the more surprising if one considers that Britain itself was once the industrial centre of the world. At that time, there was also an industrial class from which impulses spread to all others. But today, one looks for this class in vain. What has happened?

This is a terminological minefield, to be negotiated looking neither to left nor right. It is the minefield of class. There are at least three ways in which social groups, called classes, acquire their position and self-confidence. One is by inheritance, not only of a name, but of wealth and power as well. The second is through property, or professional qualifications, or political power, self-acquired. The third is by the work of one's hands, and perhaps the dependence on those in charge which one shares with many others. The riddle of British society is the weakness of the second of these groups. It is not that it does not exist; but the values with which it is normally associated – ambition and hard work, thrift and the desire to achieve more – are strangely weak. The middle class itself has settled into an older mould.

This was not always the case. Tawney is by no means wrong when he says that 'England is the country in which the middle classes triumphed earliest', though he may not have been fully aware of the ambiguity of the following statement that they 'became established most securely'.[11] Established, indeed! Historians and novelists alike have depicted the rising middle classes of Victorian Britain. But then their rise stopped, or rather, they became established in ways reminiscent more of upper-class traditions than of a self-confident middle class. E. M. Forster makes the point that while the English middle class 'strangled the aristocracy', it remained 'haunted by the ghost of its victim', and 'has never been able to build itself an appropriate home'.[12] Bertrand Russell, in his impish way, went even further and claimed that 'the concept of the gentleman was invented by the aristocracy to keep the middle classes in order'.[13] And here should be recalled Alfred Marshall's indictment of the sons of successful industrialists and merchants who desert the life of hard work and thrift for the greener pastures of a gentrified existence.[14]

In part, the causes of such developments were specific and evident. There was the strange distraction of the Empire. It offered so many more opportunities for initiative than the metropolis that many ceased to do at home what they were quite prepared to do in India or Malaya. Then, too, there was an unusual structure of ownership. Insofar as the old middle class draws its confidence from the property which it has acquired, Britain has made its life difficult. Small business ceased to play a dynamic role in Britain's economy at an early date. Farming declined to a minimum; and small industries merged and merged. Even today, many a small business is actually started up with a view, once it has been successful, to merging with a big firm. For many years, small has not been beautiful in Britain. There is a connection here between the stunting of economic growth at the turn of the century and the loss of dynamism by the middle class. Britain's middle class, too, became stunted compared to that of other countries. It settled down to enjoy its achievements rather than to set the tone for the rest.

This is clearly not the whole truth. The professional classes at least remained an important group from Victorian times to the present. Also there is some small business. And of course there is the new middle class of office workers of many grades. But none of these alter the fact that

Britain's class structure is lacking a dynamic centre. There is a middle class, but in a strange way it is like everybody else; in that sense, other groups and older values have won the day. In the United States, all men were alike when they came, or at any rate this was their theory. They had to make a living by their own work, and by exploiting the unlimited opportunities of the continent. By undertaking the risky journey across the Atlantic at all, they had shown an initiative which was not necessarily characteristic of those whom they left behind. In the New World, this spirit was kept alive. Thus the tone was set by those who succeeded by their own efforts. There was no gentry to emulate; Britain's gentry had naturally stayed at home. Similarly there was no working class in the sense of a self-confident and solidary group, for everyone strove to get ahead. Not status, but money determined where people were, and unlike status, money could be earned. It can be described as a rat-race, but also as individual advancement; either way, the achievement of the individual was both the cause and the objective of people's ambitions. In Britain, on the other hand, what one was mattered, not what one had achieved. At any rate, this was so once the new industrial class had climbed the ladder of success.

In Germany, by contrast, the story of modernisation was more complicated. At first, the new industrial class strove to be accepted by an older military-agrarian elite. Being a 'lieutenant in the reserves' was the ambition of many a successful businessman. But over time, and more particularly since the 1930s, the old ruling groups disappeared from sight. After the Second World War, West Germany became what some have called a 'levelled-in middle-class society'. Differences of income, education and social standing remained, to be sure; but the dominant values were the same for all. They are not so much about the way one lives as about how one gets there. A nice home, a few glasses of beer with friends in the evenings, watching a football match on Saturdays, a Mercedes or at least a Volkswagen to move about in, holidays in Fuerteventura and the like, are not unknown in Britain. But to add a garage first, then a sauna, then a swimming pool to one's home, or to go to Fuerteventura one year, but to Mombasa the next, and to Penang the third, or rather to have to do these things in order to keep up with the Joneses; in this, Germany is different. If by 'middle-class' values is meant dynamic values, the need to do better all the time, then Germany is middle-class and Britain is not.

Indeed, Britain's class structure is curiously static. This is why some say that it is not a class structure at all, but one of estates. 'God made them high or lowly, and order'd their estate . . .' One is upper class, or working class, or middle class; one does not try to be something else all the time. Or if one does, one suffers. If this is so, then the essentially static values of the old upper class have won the day in Britain. They have spread, first to the working class, then to the middle class, or perhaps the other way round; but they have not been diluted, let alone replaced, by the ambitions and achievements of an industrial middle class.

All this is probably changing today. In the 1960s, John Goldthorpe and David Lockwood were still able to show that the 'affluent worker' was really not very different from his less affluent historical predecessor; he knew where he belonged and what he had to do.[15] Nancy Mitford and others showed, in a slightly more flippant way, the same for the upper classes, whose affluence was even then under threat.[16] Since then, the working class has shrunk, and the upper class has diminished in importance. By sheer weight of numbers, the middle class has gained ground. This is not to say, however, that the fundamentally static character of the layers of social standing has changed. True, more people have moved from one group to the other than before. This has affected individuals as well as society. But underneath it all one can still detect the traces of a world in which being somebody is more important than becoming somebody, one which was dominated not by a rising middle class but by estates which have their own established ways, and which are loath to change them even if others regard them as 'posh', or 'disgusting', or even 'non-U'.

The minefield which we have entered now is more than one of terminology. Non-industrial values, a characteristic notion of work, the impractical nature of education, the rise and fall of a dynamic middle class, and the ossification of an immobile layer-cake of social standing, are all manifestations of that most difficult of all British issues, the issue of class. Is it the fact that Britain is class-ridden which explains the British disease? Is British society unique in its continuing emphasis on class? What does the frequent reference to class in discussions of Britain mean in any case? It is essential to look still more closely at the subject which has confused so many.

Chapter Six
A MATTER OF INEQUALITY?

Proponents of the view that what is wrong with Britain is class are not hard to find. 'As long as you maintain that damned class-ridden society of yours you will never get out of your mess,' the German Chancellor Schmidt is reported to have said during an official visit in 1975. It is more surprising to find someone who argues the opposite case, as Peter Bauer does, who quotes Helmut Schmidt and then proceeds to call this notion 'misconceived'. It ignores, he says, 'simple and undisputed facts of British history and of British social, economic and political life'. Bauer's essay, *Class on the Brain*, is concerned with 'the cost of a British obsession'.[1]

Class – obsession or reality? In the first instance, there are of course economic inequalities in Britain as in all other countries. This is a matter 'of course', because a society in which such differences do not exist has not yet been invented; and what is more, if it were to be invented, it would almost certainly be one of terror and illiberty. Economic inequalities have often been described. In recent years, such descriptions have generally been based on material provided by the Royal Commission on the Distribution of Income and Wealth.[2]

The facts are clear and beyond dispute. The richest one per cent takes home about as much as the poorest twenty per cent, though the share of the top one per cent has declined in recent decades. The reason for this is that the number of self-employed has declined and the overwhelming majority of people now work for others for a living. The same trend can be observed with respect to wealth, though inequalities of wealth are still more pronounced than those of income. In 1975, the top one per cent of the total population owned a greater share of the country's private wealth than the bottom eighty per cent. Such figures can be analysed in a variety of ways, depending on one's point of view. One can, for example, conclude from them, with A. H. Halsey, that 'class . . . remains fundamental to stratification in Britain' (though Halsey adds that it 'does not tell us the whole story').[3] The more important point, however, is that there is nothing specifically British about economic inequalities. They exist in all modern societies, indeed in all societies. They are no more pronounced in Britain than in comparable countries. It is not these inequalities which explain the unique features of British life.

The same point can be made for what has come to be called social mobility, that is, people's opportunities for moving up economically and socially, or conversely, dropping down. In recent decades, more people have moved up than down, because there has been a general improvement in economic and social conditions. As a result (as John Goldthorpe and A. H. Halsey have shown in their studies of *Social Mobility in Britain*[4]), the lower classes have declined in proportional terms, and the middle classes have grown. Peter Bauer makes much of social mobility. Indeed, the core of his argument is that 'Wolsey was the son of a butcher; Queen Elizabeth I was descended from a serf'. Britain is anything but a 'closed or even caste society'; it is 'a variegated but open and mobile society'[5]. But then, this too is true of all industrial societies.

However, looked at more closely, there are two features of this debate which are specifically British. One is brought out, involuntarily perhaps, by Peter Bauer. He likes to quote examples of people rising right to the top, to what he calls the 'upper classes'. This, he contends, is rather painless in Britain. 'The British upper classes usually absorb new men very easily. Indeed, the new recruits soon become indistinguishable from the class into which they have been recruited.'[6] Such openness requires a powerful and self-confident upper class, which is precisely the kind of estate that Britain has continued to possess, whereas other countries have lost it somewhere along the road to modernisation.

The other specific feature is quite different. It has to do with the opposite end of the social scale, and with poverty. Discussions of poverty are vexed by ideological preconceptions. Even a calm and self-critical author like Frank Field reaches the patently nonsensical conclusion: 'The numbers of poor have grown steadily during the post-war years although this has been a period of increasing prosperity.'[7]

Frank Field can say so only because he looks at poverty in terms of a socially acceptable standard of living, washing-machines and all, and not in absolute terms. Had he done the latter, he would have had to conclude with Shirley Williams: 'The welfare state and the publicly financed health services largely eliminated crude primary poverty.'[8] Today's poor are positively prosperous by comparison to the poor of 1945, let alone those of 1930, or indeed of 1913. But what has taken place is something different and much more worrying: the emergence of what Americans call an 'underclass'.

The underclass is the *lumpenproletariat* of contemporary societies, their 'passive rotting away', to use Marx's words. Many of its members are young. Many live (if that is the word) in inner cities. Many have no work other than an occasional part-time job. It is said that they do not want work, that they are 'unemployable'; and superficially speaking this is undoubtedly true. Members of the underclass are by and large not very good candidates for a Youth Opportunities Programme or projects of inner-city improvement. They have got used to scrounging, to petty theft and sometimes not so petty robbery, to hanging about in fleeting groups and gangs. Indeed, like the *lumpenproletariat* of old they are anything but a potential for revolution. They may be a reserve army for demonstrations and occasional riots; but otherwise they prefer to act alone or in small groups, or not to do anything at all. Yet, again like the *lumpenproletariat*, they document the inability of 'society', that is, of the rest of us, to find a place for some. In Britain, this is particularly though by no means exclusively true for young blacks. Schools bore them; jobs are not available; the police seem to have been invented to keep them down; they do not belong, and they are told so wherever they go. The underclass documents where a society draws the boundary between in and out. The fact that large numbers are, as it were, 'rotting away' below this line, is bound to leave traces. It will be an inconvenience at first, and then will begin to undermine the foundations of society. In the United States it is estimated that the underclass comprises between five and fifteen per cent of the population. Even if one assumes the lower figure for Britain, it is a significant element of deprivation and rejection.

The underclass is a specifically British phenomenon so far as coloured immigrants and their children are concerned. Otherwise, it, too, can be found all over the world. Indeed, the whole story of inequality which is so often told in Britain, and which has preoccupied so many scholars and politicians, is not unique. This is not to say that it is not important. The welfare state has enabled millions to see their citizenship rights become real. The reforms of the welfare state advocated by Frank Field in his *Inequality in Britain* make much sense if one is concerned about 'freedom, welfare and the state' (the subtitle of Field's book). But none of this explains the peculiar features of British values and British life. To this extent one cannot but agree with Peter Bauer's attempt to demolish the class argument. If economic inequality and social mobility are to be the indicators, then the differences between Britain and, say, Germany, or the United States, are not significant.

But then, perhaps, the indicators are wrong. Perhaps, economic inequality and social mobility are not what the argument is about at all. Peter Bauer has an endearing way of making the crucial point in an aside, almost in passing. Thus he says: 'British society has for centuries displayed acute awareness of fine distinctions. The difference between a C.B. and a C.B.E. is recognised to this day throughout the Civil Service, and often beyond it. Civil servants are unhappy to receive a C.B.E. when they expect a C.B., or an O.B.E. when they hope for a C.B.E. Perception of differences extends far down the social scale – witness saloon bars, lounge bars and public bars in working class pubs.'9 No-one will, I hope, expect an explanation of the difference between a Commander of the Order of Bath, and one of the Order of the British Empire. The distinction is fine indeed. But then, *fine distinctions* is perhaps a better word than class to decribe what is unique about British society. What is more, fine distinctions are not only made, but are given meaning, and turned into worlds of difference. The subtle division of labour which Adam Smith described in such memorable terms, is turned into an even more subtle division of social standing, or of belonging, and every estate resulting from this process has its own symbols, rules, and above all boundaries. Where other countries have become societies of large and overlapping categories which are all dominated by one central set of values, Britain has remained a society of fine distinctions. This is the real issue hidden behind the debate on class.

Chapter Seven
THE UPPER CLASSES, OR HOW THE TONE IS SET

The distinctions which people make may be fine, but when it comes to class they also fall into a cruder grid. There is the ancient line between the estates of 'those who work' and 'those who don't work' or, in somewhat less invidious terms, the 'working class' and the 'upper class', not to forget the 'middle class' between them which has successfully done its work and arrived. Actually, the fact that these terms are often used in the plural – 'working classes', 'middle classes', 'upper classes' – is a hint that within them, there are other, finer distinctions. These are regional and professional, sometimes denominational, but above all they draw lines between layers which make up a subtle structure of status. There is a very old, an old, and a more recent upper class; there is an upper middle, a middle middle and a lower middle class; there is a skilled, a semi-skilled and an unskilled working class – and this is only the beginning of such distinctions. Yet the more inclusive notions retain their meaning.

Class in Britain is like a layer cake in which clear distinctions can be drawn between the bottom of the cake, the jam in the middle, and the chocolate on top (if such a concoction holds together). Its characteristics are, in the modern world, unique. For one thing, the differences between the layers are not gradual. If social standing is based on money, then distinctions are statistical inventions, such as those between people earning less than £5,000, and those earning more. In Britain, however, distinctions are real. It is easy to identify the layers, however thin they may be as one gets nearer the top of the cake. Such qualitative distinctions do not rule out movement from one layer to the other. But they mean that moving is visible, and perhaps rather more painful than Peter Bauer admits. One moves, and acquires a whole new culture as one moves. Queen Elizabeth I may have been descended from a serf, but she certainly did not behave like one. The metaphor of the cake also means, most importantly perhaps, that there is no one dynamic element in the whole. In particular – to abandon the metaphor – the middle class is not significantly different from others in its acceptance of its place. Moreover, there still is an upper class. In most developed countries, there is nobody left who would describe himself as 'upper class'; everybody is 'middle class' somehow, at most 'upper middle class'. Perhaps there is not as much left of the upper class in Britain as some seem to think, either. And yet the tone of the whole edifice of status is set by the memory, and to some extent the reality, of this class.

Who comprise it? One is tempted to say that they are the backwoodsmen of the House of Lords, those who rarely emerge from their country seats although they are members of the Second Chamber. But that would be to underestimate them. A foreign newspaper argued that the division between 'hardliners' and 'wets' in Margaret Thatcher's cabinet coincided exactly with that between middle-class and upper-class ministers;[1] but if one considers the names, the point is more striking than plausible. Characteristically, one has to move from people to abstractions, to how they are rather than who they are, to make the case.

Harry and Caroline Stow-Crat (as Jilly Cooper names the exemplars of the upper class in her amusing book on *Class*[2]) do not care much about money, though it is of course nice to have it. Not seeming to care about possessions is in fact one of the misleading traits of Britain's upper class, given the wealth of many of its members. However, theirs is often inactive wealth; their castles and mansions cost much to keep up and are not easily sold. The Stow-Crats do not care much about working too hard, either; they hate to put themselves out. Not that they sit about doing nothing – though they do not mind that from time to time; but really hard work is simply not done. Work is for them a combination of dabbling in the running of things, whether as non-executive directors, members of boards or gentleman farmers, and of voluntary work for charities and other benevolent purposes. It is not surprising that education has a particular, and limited, meaning for them. It is not so much a training in specifics, as a confirmation of status and a preparation for the behaviour that goes with it. If caning is 'necessary' to achieve this purpose, so be it; but engineering is certainly not necessary. Even so, they know how to enjoy their lives. And they are recognisable, at least to the English. They speak in their own ways; their accent is unmistakable. To the Continental, the contrived negligence of their appearance is a little surprising; but it too is a part of a style.

Yet the relaxed and generous style of Britain's upper class must not be misunderstood. It is after all the style of an upper class: one knows who belongs and who does not, and one also knows that those who belong regard power as an almost natural attribute. If they are amateurs in engineering, or even economics, they are professionals when it comes to running things. Whether by foreign standards, or even by those of domestic success, they are very good at running industry, for example, is another matter. Fine distinctions are of little use in a modern economy. But in Britain they are understood, and the upper-class *dilettante* continues to be accepted as a director of companies or a cabinet minister.

Now it would be quite wrong to give the impression that the power of Britain's upper class has remained unopposed. The rising middle class of Victorian Britain presented it with an enormous challenge. Indeed, it may have won the battle for civil liberties against the upper class. But it did not win the battle for social domination. Today it is permissible to wonder whether it wanted to win. Britain's middle class turned out to be curiously acquiescent. It settled down to a position of comfortable security, not at the top, but not anywhere near the bottom either. Insofar as its members exercised power, they tended to borrow the values and perspectives of those who had held power before them. Their social interests, too, resembled those of the upper classes, if at a somewhat lesser level. They had, and have, a cottage, not a country seat, and a flat, not a mansion, in town, or rather a nice house with a garden in the stockbroker belt. Clubs and cricket and leisure and friends and education and many other pleasures of life make up their existence. It is a pleasant one, and this is precisely the point: England's middle class is not harassed and ambitious, but happy and acquiescent. It is not a ruling middle class nor one that is driven by a ceaseless hunger for more; it is the English middle class. More than anything else, it represents the values already discussed in several contexts, which will be of concern throughout this book.

Thus, the upper classes managed to resist the first challenge to their rule. They absorbed some of the challengers, and imposed the values of a static world of estates on the others. But this was not the end of the story. More recently, at least two significant groups have renewed the challenge from the middle; and it may well be that unlike their historical predecessors they are going to win the day.

One of these groups illustrates better than most the layer-cake condition of status in Britain; it is the estate of those who have made it through education. The word meritocracy was coined by a British author, Michael Young.[3] But the fact of advancing along the ladder of education to the top is much more widespread in other countries. Moreover, in Britain, social advancement even by educational achievement is painful. There is a moving chapter in Richard Hoggart's *Uses of Literacy* about the 'scholarship boy', the working class lad who has brains and who therefore steps on the ladder, first of educational, then of professional success.[4] But his success is tempered with tears. Hoggart describes the working class living room. 'Mother is ironing, the wireless is on, someone is singing a snatch of a song or Father says intermittently what comes into his head. The boy has to cut himself off mentally, so as to do his homework, as well as he can.'[5] Cutting himself off in a concrete, almost physical sense, is the beginning of a very much larger cutting-off. As the scholarship boy grows older, he comes to live in worlds which are quite different from those of his parents. And as he does so, he is torn; indeed being torn becomes the very essence of his life. 'He has left his class, at least in spirit, by being in certain ways unusual; and he is still unusual in another class, too tense and over-wound.'[6]

Hoggart wrote this in the 1950s, that is, before the great educational revolution of the 1960s. This revolution has led among other things to a significant increase in the number of scholarship boys. There are now so many scholarship boys, and girls for that matter, that they have begun to form an estate of their own. This is a strange, indeed a strangely unhappy, estate; but then unhappiness is a precondition of any struggle for power. One can call it the educational class, because many scholarship boys and girls have never left the world of schools and colleges and universities. They combine radical politics with *petit bourgeois* life styles which are only intermittently dented by the scruffy appearance which has become a status symbol of its own. They dislike the upper class as the acquiescent middle class of old. They like to glorify the working class, though not without making sure that their distance from it is never forgotten. They live in communities of equals. They have even begun to create their own political party, by pushing working people to the outskirts of the Labour Party. Thus their challenge to the old ruling class is one from the opposite end rather than from nearby.

The second challenge has other sources. There is another unhappy group in the middle which also believes in radical change, though its programme is rather different. It would be invidious to describe this group as that of estate agents, other semi-professionals, and supervisors. It is located socially right on the boundary between blue-collar and white-collar groups. What it wants is economic progress. It does not care much about education, and still less about the educational class, though it accepts specialist training and practical interests as useful. On the other hand, it does care about increasing productivity, cutting welfare, promoting growth and advancing individually. In a sense, this somewhat undefined class – or is it a mere assemblage of unrelated individuals? indeed is it all of us to some extent? – is the modern version of the Victorian middle class. It is dissatisfied, therefore striving for new horizons, and clearly representing a different world from the upper class which has ruled Britain for so long.

The vehicle for this group's bid for power is the Conservative Party. Two successive leaders of the party, Edward Heath and Margaret Thatcher, have in fact, if not intentionally, launched an outright attack on the values of the traditional upper classes as well as the acquiescent middle class. We shall see that by implication at least they have attacked the traditional working classes as well. Mrs Thatcher's demand for an ethic of hard work and of thrift, for deferred gratification and individual competition, does not appeal to traditional British values; it involves a demand for radical change. It is therefore no accident that she likes to invoke foreign examples, such as Ludwig Erhard's Germany with its economic miracle. It is also no accident that some of her harshest critics are to be found among the traditional estates of the country; to this extent the foreign newspaper which confronted 'hardline' middle-class and 'wet' upper-class ministers was right.

However, the fact that the tone of government, and of a Tory government at that, can be set by what are distinctly modern middle-class values, is bound to mark a change. This change affects the very heart of upper-class domination, the monopoly by this estate of social and political power. One of many expressions of the survival of pre-modern values in modern Britain is the style of rule. Whether in government, or industry, or indeed in any other organisation, the way in which power is exercised in Britain may be effective, but it must be described as authoritarian. Once a chairman has summarised a discussion, it is simply not done to point out that the summary is biassed towards the chairman's personal preferences. Voting is the exception rather than the rule in most bodies. There is not only the distance between those in charge and those who have to follow which is symbolised by directors' dining rooms in industry, but also a very considerable asymmetry between whoever is in the chair and the rest. For those at the top, this is bearable; they will all be in the chair at some time. Still, when Harold Wilson informed Barbara Castle that as of this morning he had appointed another Secretary of State for Health and Social Services, he acted as few Prime Ministers in other democratic countries could afford to do. The ultimate right of the Prime Minister, that of dissolving Parliament and calling an election, is yet another illustration of the fact that democracy as understood elsewhere has made but halting progress in Britain. This is even more strongly the case when one looks at the secrecy with which most decisions are shrouded. 'A strong elitist strain runs through the dominant layers of British life,' says Bernard Nossiter in this connection; and one can quarrel with the way he puts it, but his point is taken. 'They see themselves as guardians of a society that cannot bear too much information, an over-exposure to truth.'[7]

But this too is changing; here, too, the influence of a demanding new middle class can be felt. Perhaps the new Conservatives have not fully realised yet that one of the consequences of their departure from tradition is bound to be the extension of what in most countries would be called democracy. For the moment, it is in any case the other demanding new middle class, that of the left, which makes most of the running. Leaving aside the tactical function of its demands within the Labour Party, it is not always easy to see why they should be wrong. After all, why should a sitting MP have the automatic right to remain the constituency candidate forever unless he or she is removed? Why should there not be more freedom of information? In a sense, the scholarship boys of the left have become the spearhead of middle-class progress, however reluctant the inhabitants of the stockbroker belt may be to admit it.

The change described would be neither dramatic nor particularly painful. Indeed, its effects would be fairly predictable. It would mean that Britain's upper class would retreat still further, and that its values would become increasingly irrelevant. In most countries, this has happened a long time ago. There is no need for legislation which makes .carrying titled names illegal (as in Austria) to bring about this result. It is perfectly viable to have, by divorce and remarriage as well as by adding the title to the name rather than just passing it on to the eldest son, an ever-increasing number of people carrying aristocratic names (as in Germany). There are already signs of the growing irrelevance of the old gentry. The number of backwoodsmen among the peers of the realm is large, and Life Peers are hardly Stow-Crats. Moreover, the sons of the backwoodsmen as a rule work for their living. Yet the progress of the aggressive middle classes is slow and, what is more, uncertain. So far as the definition of what the British stand for is concerned, it is still more likely to be borrowed from an older tradition. The old estates linger on, and are likely to do so for some time.

Chapter Eight
THE WORKING CLASSES, OR HOW THINGS HOLD TOGETHER

It takes two to make up 'them' and 'us', and so far it is largely the upper half of the balance that has been discussed. Jilly Cooper calls her working-class couple Mr and Mrs Definitely-Disgusting. She thereby not only shows whom she regards as 'them', but takes a middle-class view; the traditional upper classes would never have called the working class 'definitely disgusting'. Actually, there is a strange symmetry between the two classes. Jilly Cooper knows this: 'Anyone studying the English Class system will have noticed certain similarities between the extreme upper and lower classes: their toughness, xenophobia, their indifference to public opinion, their passion for racing and gambling, and their fondness for plain speaking and plain untampered food.'[1] Leaving xenophobia and gambling on one side, the important point is that there is a working class at all. The English like the games which 'they', those at the top, play, the distinctions between 'U' and 'non-U', napkins and serviettes, between those who have made it and those who have not quite; but these merely illustrate the many layers of the middle and upper estates. Apart from those at the top, there is another group which is definitely 'U' in its own way, or rather, which is 'us' in Richard Hoggart's distinction between 'them' and 'us': that is the working class.[2]

I cannot claim to have any first-hand knowledge of Britain's working class. There are occasional glimpses, to be sure; there is a sense of whether what one reads rings true or not; but otherwise I am dependent on others for what I know. This is a reason for caution. It is perhaps itself worth considering. In part my ignorance betrays the way of life of the alien who is in charge of an institution and therefore more likely to move in the middle and upper reaches of society. In part it may be a comment on the hermetic quality of the working class, that is, the fact that it holds together in ways which make it difficult for the outsider to look in. In part, though, I am simply surprised by the phenomenon. On the Continent, the expression 'working class' is most likely to be used by intellectual agitators; those who actually belong to it would either describe themselves as 'middle class', or abstain from any description. Everybody likes to call himself a 'worker', or at any rate to indicate that he works, and works hard, for a living; but the notion of a working class which has its own boundaries and rules and symbols seems strange to most Frenchmen or Germans, or, for that matter, Americans.

The underlying reason why Continentals or Americans find the British working class strange has to do with what has been identified as solidarity as a value. The working class epitomises what such solidarity means. Richard Hoggart's description of working-class life is relevant. Hoggart begins by stressing 'the group-sense', 'the sense of group warmth' which is characteristic of the working class. It is perhaps not surprising. 'The friendly group tradition seems to me to have its strength initially from the ever-present evidence, in the close, huddled, intimate conditions of life, that we are, in fact, all in the same position.' Many other attitudes follow from this sense of belonging. It will not do to be different. 'Love, friends, a good home', and a decent life with others, are more important than money and power, let alone success.[3]

There is something strangely passive about working class values. 'Live and let live' is after all not a principle of active progress, although it is one of liberty. Even what has been called the reactionary quality of the working class is essentially passive. It is true that there are working-class housing estates which their inhabitants and their political representatives have deliberately kept 'clean' (as they put it), that is, free of coloured people. Working-class people have no more time for blacks than they do for women's rights or any other of the highfalutin' ideas of modern progressives. But in intention at least, there is nothing nasty in such attitudes; they are, rather, defensive. 'The group . . . works against the idea of change,' suggests Hoggart. Even someone from a town only forty miles away may for many years find it difficult to be accepted in his new locality. Solidarity, neighbourliness, friendliness, gentleness are all virtues which it is easy to extend within a familiar environment; but if the environment changes, those virtues can rapidly begin to evaporate.

In any case, we must beware of painting too idyllic a picture of the working class. There is not only another side to the coin as we have so far presented it; there are also changes which have taken place and which may have destroyed traditional working-class attitudes irrevocably. Moreover, the seeds of this destruction lay in the attitudes themselves. For there is a simple and yet infinitely complicated question: how can a society hold together in which there are two very disparate and widely distant classes? How do the two cultures merge into one? What is the role of the middle classes in this process? What is the source of social cohesion in Britain – and what has happened to it in recent years?

To explain this, it is not enough to repeat that the upper and the lower ends of British society have much in common. Such community is in any case more apparent than real. It is more important to point out that as upper-class values involve a 'natural' affinity to rule, and middle-class values a posture of service to the rulers, so working-class attitudes involve a strong, if reluctant, element of obedience. The distinction between 'them' and 'us' is no joke. '"They" are "the people at the top", "the higher-ups", the people who give you your dole, call you up, tell you to go to war, fine you, made you split the family in the thirties to avoid a reduction in the Means Test allowance, "get yer in the end", "aren't really to be trusted", "talk posh", "are all twisters really", "never tell yer owt" (e.g. about a relative in hospital), "clap yer in clink", "will do y' down if they can", "summons yer", "are all in a click [clique] together", "treat y' like muck".'[4] There is a strange mixture of acceptance and resentment in this list of working-class phrases which Richard Hoggart has put together. Edward Shils has expressed this ambiguity in unambiguous terms. The class system of Britain, he says, demanded 'a lot both from those who were its obvious beneficiaries and those who were its obvious victims'. The beneficiaries, those on top, were born and bred not only to rule but also to accept the discipline of institutions. 'It was a discipline which was integral to ruling.' Those at the bottom on the other hand were not only subject to this rule, but had to accept their subjection. 'From those at the bottom, [the class system] demanded more than obedience, it demanded respectability. Respectability entailed not only self-restraint, it entailed deference to one's betters, which involved self-derogation.'[5]

This too may sound somewhat old-fashioned today. Moreover it needs some translation. Perhaps the way to begin is to state clearly that social cohesion in Britain, as elsewhere, was in the first instance brought about by rule, that is, by the exercise of authority by some, and obedience by many. Rule in this sense invariably generates resentment.

In the past, Britain was by no means a gentle and non-violent society. On the contrary, the early part of the nineteenth century was a period of a great deal of public violence, with soldiers shooting workers and workers rising to burn and to loot and generally to sock the rich. Such violence continued well into the later parts of the century. Moreover, public and private violence in the form of revolts quenched by force on the one hand, and violent crime on the other, came to be equally prevalent. It would be wrong to project the more peaceful experience of recent decades into the more distant past. Brixton and Toxteth are not new; they are a revival of an older British response to the burden of social cohesion.

Yet it is true that, at least from a certain historical point onwards, the cohesion of Britain was not simply brought about by force and obedience. Dare one suggest that, in this respect as in that of economic decline, the First World War marks the crucial dividing line? However, dating the process is less important than explaining how it happened that social cohesion in Britain came to be a matter of self-discipline and voluntary acceptance rather than the disciplining of the disobedient by soldiers and policemen. Here, the very static nature of Britain's class system may have been turned to advantage. We have described the upper class as relaxed, the middle class as acquiescent, and the working class as essentially passive. This is not the stuff from which disruption is made. Yet cohesion requires more. It requires a glue which binds social groups together. Perhaps this is one of the few points at which Britain's acquiescent middle class set the tone after all. The very fact that it had ceased to contest for power in the land at an early date made it a model of coming to terms with things. The old middle class of Britain was not only the link between 'them' and 'us' – for working-class people its members obviously belonged to 'them', though for upper-class people they were 'non-U' – but above all a model of the voluntary acceptance of the discipline which is necessary for holding things together. The middle class may have been but the notary of the contract of social cohesion; even so, without it, the contract would not have been concluded.

It is worth recalling the effect of this contract. It meant that people exercised self-discipline in the observance of rules. This in turn meant that there were fewer rules than in countries in which every other thing is *verboten*, and above all that the police was not the ever-present armed hand of the state, but a peaceful and friendly force essentially there to help rather than to control. It is hard to exaggerate the significance of the fact that the British police did not, and very largely still do not, carry weapons. But self-discipline and a friendly police were only a part of the story. Non-violence, not using one's elbows but queuing, protecting the integrity of others by being kind to them, that is, all the civic virtues for which Britain has been so widely acclaimed, belong to the same story. Again, there were no institutions to bring about the result; it simply happened, as if people had discovered for themselves that this was the most civilised way to live. It was an insular way to be sure. Just as a severe quarantine imposed on the import of animals has managed to keep out rabies, so insular patterns of life protected society against 'social rabies'. This was achieved not only by the psychological quarantine which makes every traveller at Dover and Heathrow feel it a great privilege to be allowed in, but by the protective strength of the attitude itself. Britain's self-discipline and kindness were infectious, even though zebra crossings never came to work in other countries into which they were soon introduced, and enthralled foreign visitors were soon using their elbows again when on returning home they found that queuing meant simply that one never got what one wanted.

In this connection, the 'Spirit of Dunkirk' has its proper place. It is true that in the normal course of events, social cohesion has not meant unity of purpose but acceptance of difference. The rules of the social contract remained formal, such as being kind, not trespassing, and so on. But every now and again, living and letting live could turn into a joint effort to pull the whole country together. There was, and undoubtedly is, something about being British which the alien can only guess at. A BBC radio discussion in which I took part was produced by a 1956 refugee from Hungary who had of course since been 'naturalised' (*naturalised*, that is, brought to his natural state!) and thus become British. The politicians who took part in the discussion spoke a lot about the delights of being British. As we left the studio, the producer remarked: 'Isn't it strange how you all praise this country, and yet I am the only one here who is British by choice rather than by the accident of birth?' One of the politicians, a well-known man who shall nevertheless remain nameless here, turned round in anger and nearly screamed: 'Accident? Being born British is not an accident!'

Once again, an important point had to be made in the past tense: the idyllic picture of social cohesion by voluntary agreement. Today, this is, if not broken, then at any rate dented. There are, to be sure, great differences between small country places in which the old virtues are still alive, and the cities. Indeed, every time one leaves London one is struck by how much of the old Britain is still there to see and to enjoy. Perhaps it can be said that the stronger the old, acquiescent middle class has remained, the more intact the contract of voluntary discipline and restraint is likely to be. Yet it is crumbling. The list of riots has by now become long; and riots are only the most painful expression of the fact that something seems to have gone awry. What is it?

Many have asked this question, yet few have given a convincing answer. And indeed convincing answers are hard to find. One can point to the fact that modernity has at last caught up with Britain. Here, too, the traditional ligatures of family and class, religion and place of origin no longer bind. The beautiful balance which held the country together has been upset. Social rabies, at least, has invaded Britain's shores. One can relate this unfortunate occurrence to the decline of the acquiescent middle class of old, or rather, the rise of more aggressive middle-class groups which demand their place in the sun and espouse unfamiliar values. The remnants of the established heirs of the Victorian industrial class are still there to see, but they no longer hold the rest of the layer cake together. One can also point to the unhappy position of the young, the sixteen to twenty-year-olds, and in large cities those fifteen, fourteen, even thirteen as well. They are no longer contained by their families of origin, and not yet enmeshed by their jobs and their own families. The gap into which they fall is both an insult and a temptation. It is an insult in that it tells them that society does not need them. It is a temptation, encouraging them to go their own way, to roam, to scrounge, to steal, to squat, to mug. They feel they have been abandoned by the rest. One can point to unemployment in general. It is a disorienting experience, especially in a work society. As long as one's material well-being and one's self-confidence depend on having a job, those who are out of employment are lost, and are bound to doubt the fairness of the society around them. The same is true for those many others who fear that they too might soon be out of a job, or who merely resent the fact that there is widespread unemployment.

Then there is the vexing and unresolved issue of race. It has been mentioned once or twice, and even now it is impossible to deal with it in detail. Let there be no doubt, though, that coming to terms with its new citizens from Asia, West Africa and the West Indies is the single most difficult and important task before British society today. They number between two and three million. Exact figures are not known, because both immigrants and their advocates have successfully resisted a census question which would have made it possible to identify them. Most have come between the mid-1950s and the mid-1970s, either because they had to leave their home countries, or because they hoped for greater life chances in Britain, or both. When they came, they were British citizens as of right. In this sense they are a late remnant of Britain's imperial tradition. Insofar as this imperial tradition is associated above all with the upper classes, the new immigration could be called the last present by the upper class of the country to its working class. For not surprisingly, most of the newcomers joined the poorer groups of society. The present was a Trojan horse. As we have seen, the working class was not eager to embrace its new fellows. For once, the 'close, huddled, intimate conditions of life' led to demarcation rather than solidarity. At trade union meetings, or Labour Party conferences, few if any Asians and West Indians are to be seen. For those on top, or even the middle class, the problem is much less immediate. They can afford to repress the issue, until it stares them in the face in the form of attacks by skinheads on successful Asian small businessmen, or riots by West Indians against the police.

For so far Britain has shown a singular inability to cope with its new citizens. The Home Affairs Committee of the House of Commons has criticised the Home Office for its 'essentially passive role of spectator' in matters of race relations: it has also taken a dim view of Community Relations Councils and predicted that Liverpool is only a beginning, 'a grim warning to all of Britain's cities that racial disadvantage cannot be expected to disappear by natural causes'. But how does it disappear? On this, the Home Affairs Committee was divided. The majority wanted, among other things, employers to monitor black employees to make sure that there was no discrimination and that appropriate jobs are found for them. A minority called this 'positive discrimination', and objected because it 'runs totally counter to our traditional even-handed approach to British citizens regardless of the colour of their skins'.[6] This sounds good – but is there any sign of such even-handedness in the case of race?

Lord Scarman, in his remarkable report on *The Brixton Disorders*, provides much evidence that such even-handedness does not exist. He casts some doubt on the role of the police in areas in which ethnic minorities are concentrated. He has a great deal to say about the conditions of disadvantage under which these minorities live. While Lord Scarman is at pains not to impute discriminatory motives to police, government agencies, or large social groups, he notes that 'it would be disastrous . . . if there were to be any wider doubt than at present exists among the ethnic minorities about the will of Government, employers, trade union leaders and others in positions of authority to see [the elimination of discrimination] through'. Lord Scarman is less hesitant than the Home Affairs Committee to conclude that 'if the balance of racial disadvantage is to be redressed, as it must be, positive action is required'.[7]

No one doubts the difficulties in the way of redressing discrimination. These begin with the fact that the one word 'race' or even the notion of ethnic minority, in fact covers a multitude of issues. For one thing, there are significant differences between Asians, who manage to find a place for themselves in economic terms, but remain culturally separate, and West Indians. Asians are an almost obvious object of racist wrath on the part of what in the United States would be called 'poor white trash'. West Indians, on the other hand, though culturally less obviously different, steel bands and all, are not only black, but are said to have a different attitude to work. While they are more likely to become members of the working class, even British workers tend to regard them as rather happy-go-lucky. In any case, race and class are superimposed in a variety of ways. Race riots and class riots are almost indistinguishable. Similarly, it is hard to separate race and unemployment as reasons for disaffection. All that is clear is that many of the new immigrants belong to what has been described as the underclass. In this sense, too, they document a strange inability of the rest to cope.

But then, what does coping mean? It is in the first instance a matter of attitudes. There are not many multiracial societies which work, and even fewer free societies which are multiracial and work. Accepting someone obviously different is all the more difficult in a world in which there is a new longing for identity within circumscribed social spaces. Thus, Peregrine Worsthorne's demand for the assimilation of the new citizens requires a major revival of traditional virtues. It also requires imagination. Making a class of blacks and Asians write the sentence, 'The Vikings are our ancestors' is clearly not good enough; yet the example is genuine. A new Britain will have to emerge from the process of accepting those who came and have nowhere else to go, and in particular the children of immigrants born in this country. There may even be a need to stimulate necessary changes by doing what some MPs understandably find distateful, that is, by engaging in some 'affirmative action' in order to make sure that minorities are not forgotten. There certainly will have to be a re-examination of policing and of official attitudes in general. But in the end, one hopes that older attitudes prevail. In an article entitled 'A Paradox for the Creatures of Empire', the former Prime Minister of Jamaica, Michael Manley, offers a warm description of Britain's way of life and says that 'the British have a genius for creating a neighbourly environment, even in one of the biggest cities in the world'; but then he adds the sad and pertinent question: 'What is the use of a gift for living if it cannot extend the comfort of its warmth to a black skin?'[8] What indeed?

But so far, signs of change are few and far between. Instead, there is turmoil. The embarrassment of race has compounded the uncertainties and self-doubts created by unemployment, the unsettled young, aggressive new middle-class groups, and the forward march of modernity in general. In this climate, it is hardly surprising that people begin to wonder about yesterday's assumptions, that they try to test them, indeed shake them, only to find that they crumble. People have another look at accepted values and virtues, and they soon discover that the Emperor has no clothes. For self-discipline, voluntary kindness, non-violence, and all the other British virtues are highly precarious. There is no real reason why one should behave in this way, except social control, the fact that all others behave in the same way and one feels watched by them. Perhaps, being disciplined and kind makes not only others, but also oneself feel better; though in the end, some may discover that while these virtues make others feel better, it is much more exciting not to behave in accepted ways. So one stops doing what is done; and right away, all hell breaks loose. A society which has relied on self-discipline and social control for so long is quite unprepared for the violence of selfishness and the uncontrolled expression of resentment. The picture of Liverpool policemen facing, with inflammable shields and in an eighteenth-century battle order, small groups of vicious youths throwing petrol bombs at them, is unforgettable. It is a picture that speaks well for the institutions of Britain. But it also indicates that they are under threat.

And what does the working class have to do with things falling apart, things it has helped hold together for so long? It is not its fault, to be sure. If it is anybody's fault it is that of the new, radical middle-class groups of the left and the right. But they too are the predictable product of changes in economic conditions and social opportunities. In a sense, what is happening now is nobody's fault. But it has a working-class aspect. In fact, it could be said that changes in the size, position, character and behaviour of the working classes symbolise all other changes which have happened. To some extent, these changes, and the ways in which they are expressed, remind one of earlier battles between 'them' and 'us'. Karl Heinz Bohrer, in his analysis of the 1981 riots ('Babylon burns'), asks his readers not to make the mistake of tucking these painful phenomena away as mere results of unemployment, inner-city squalor, or even as fascism. They may be all this, and certainly action is needed to cope with the issues. But there is another aspect to them. In Bohrer's view, recent riots may be new in their style and technique, but are also an almost traditional expression of working-class attitudes. The difference is that skinheads, and, alas, West Indians, are hardly proud, confident, spokesmen of their groups, but feel threatened. 'Whereas the Teddy Boys had adapted the fashion renaissance of the Edwardian gentleman around 1953 to their specific possibilities and their tests, and the Mods had produced a British mafioso-type and worker-dandy, the Skinheads characteristically oriented themselves from the beginning to their social background which had been a matter of course for their predecessors, but which must appear threatened to them: the "working-class" world of the terraced house, the pub, the football ground and Saturday-night-Sunday-morning fun.' And again: 'The English subculture which now explodes against the culture, is in its basis proletarian, and in its mentality anti-idealistic, unintellectual, nonliterary and infinitely excessive and brutal . . . It reminds one of the wild revolts of the London mob a few years before the French Revolution when Newgate prison was stormed and troops had to be brought in. . . The proletarian subculture of West Indians and white Skinheads not only does not know the normative culture, but is confined to suffering it as "the system" which it cannot understand.' Thus, what we see today is a recurrence of history. Bohrer notes this without middle-class concern. 'It is also a piece of that proud English history which is called "freedom".'[9]

Some may disagree. Many may hope that the new unrest will go away as it has come. But it probably will not. In the meantime, more police have been armed. There are no inflammable riot shields any longer. More and more people know how to take care when there is trouble, unless they are fascinated by it and go to watch it. In a sense, British society is moving from a civilised contract of good behaviour back to the hard core of power and obedience which was always its foundation. This is a dangerous route, though one which gives people little choice. No one is deliberately taking the country down this raw and painful path; this is happening as a result of thousands of spontaneous acts by individuals. In this respect, too, Britain is going through a period in which change is inevitable, because it is already happening. Where will it end if it remains unchecked? The answer may well be gloomy. But then it must not remain unchecked. Thousands of considered acts by individuals could make sure that a new contract is built on the debris of the old. After all, there is a lot going for a country which has such recent memories of kindness and peace.

Chapter Nine
DOES CLASS MATTER?

In classical Marxian analysis, class means something rather different from the story told in these chapters: two large categories, those in charge of the means of production and those excluded from ownership, provide the reservoir of social and political organisation. The purpose of such organisation is social warfare. Thus classes become political actors. Moreover, their balance increasingly tilts in favour of the underdogs. In the end, the suppressed upset the whole structure of society in a revolution which ends the old class war. Not one of these statements describes what has happened in Britain in the last century and a half. The story of British economic and social development is a very different one indeed.

First of all, class in the Marxian sense seems curiously modern in comparison to what happened in Britain. There was a dynamic force, in the form of the group which Marx described as the bourgeoisie. Indeed, Marx took his illustrations very largely from the English experience. But even his description of the displacement of the aristocracy and the ascent to power of the bourgeoisie is not correct. In the case of Britain, one is tempted to use a very different historical analogy. Just as Rome conquered Greece, but adopted its values, so the middle class conquered industry in Victorian times, but instead of dominating society from its new vantage point, it either adopted the attitudes of an earlier upper class, or settled down to its own important, if secondary, position in a static layer-cake of social estates. Hard-working, thrifty, non-conformist industrialists, or their sons, became gentlemen, and thereby abandoned the claim to power which their peers in other countries staked so successfully. In that sense, it can be said that the principles of an older social construction came to dominate Britain again after the turmoil of the industrial revolution, with the variations which this revolution inevitably involved. Money was forgotten again, and status was remembered.

Perhaps the greatest success of those who had a stake in non-industrial values and the order of things that goes with them is to have turned the industrial working class into an estate. Its members too accepted the notion that society is about being somebody in a defined position, not about getting somewhere, let alone about turning things upside down. Thus the working class, far from being the spearhead of revolution, created its own social world which was unique in many respects, though some of its elements looked like a mirror image of the values of those on top. Of course there were conflicts betwen 'them' and 'us', but somehow these did not affect the fundamental creed of 'live and let live'. In a sense, the separateness of estates was more important than their antagonisms. This separateness protected the members of all, and allowed them a life which was decent by their own standards.

For there is a significant difference between conflicts in Britain and a class struggle *à la* Marx: in Britain, there was never an indication that the working class actually wanted to take over the reins of the country. Conflicts with those on top, riots included, were an expression of the resentment arising from a given position – but indeed one that is given, that is, one which it is impossible to get rid of, or turn upside down. If there are signs at all of something resembling a class conflict in contemporary Britain, their origin is in the new middle classes, left and right, and not in the working class. The passivity of the working class is not to be misunderstood. It certainly does not mean that workers do not want an improvement of their situation. But then, there is little disagreement between them and the other estates, and notably the upper classes: improvement is necessary. The welfare state is not so much the result of the class struggle as that of a general appreciation of needs. Characteristically, it was advanced most rapidly when the classes were closest together, during the two wars, and not as a result of pre-1914 riots, or of the General Strike of 1926.

The condition which we have described is not the Hobbesian world of Marx's nightmares; it is idyllic by comparison. And indeed Britain was idyllic by comparison to others. But this condition could not last. A. H. Halsey is quite right when he says, in his Reith Lectures on *Change in British Society*, 'that the history of the twentieth century is the history of the decay of the values and status system of Victorian

Britain'. (He is less right when he calls the estates which we have described a result of a 'reconstruction of status [which] accompanied the dissolution of the old order': the kind of status system which we have described in fact represents the old order.[1]) The old order could not last. For one thing it meant that the economic basis for the survival of all estates began to be threatened. The mixture of feudal values and industrial reality became explosive. A choice had to be made. As it happened, the older values turned out to be very strong indeed. Their strength is one of the main causes of the stunted growth of Britain's economy. But inevitably, if gradually, they lost their grip.

The ferment of change emerged, as we have seen, in the middle of the edifice of status. (Perhaps it always originates there; new social forces are successful because they begin their march on the way up rather than in a state of subjection and destitution.) Gone are the days in which scholarship boys suffer in their fathers' living rooms; gone also the days in which blue- and white-collar people were content to become gentlemen. Their life styles, their demands, and even their accents have come to dominate more and more institutions. They have also come to affect and even impress the old, acquiescent middle class.

Thus it can be said that all three estates of old are declining. In the case of the upper classes, this leaves little more than a nostalgic memory. Thousands go to visit stately homes each Sunday, and those who continue to live in their private apartments are not ashamed to take the pennies of the tourists. In the case of the middle classes, the decline of some means a sharpening of the social and political ambitions of others. The direction of such ambitions is not always clear, though Tony Benn and Margaret Thatcher speak for the new middle classes and demonstrate their radical temper. Once a working class perceives itself to be in decline, it becomes disaffected and violent. Nationalism, protectionism, racism and many other ugly -isms have their social home in this group.

Yet the values which are threatened by such changes are by no means simply quaint, let alone irrelevant. Working to live is a part of a dignified human existence in freedom, and solidarity provides ligatures which are missing in most parts of the modern world. All the attractions of British life which are such an endless source of pleasure, of humour, of emulation, have their origin in what some would call the survival of status in a world of class. Even conflicts do not serve to overturn the existing order, but to affirm the status of each and all. Conflicts are won and lost with some grace. Or rather, they were; because again there is change.

Old England and its attitudes could not last. One will be able to find its traces for some considerable time, but these are mere traces. There is change. With change, there is confusion. Conflicts become uglier, because the rules of the game are deliberately violated, or perhaps forgotten. Conservatives no longer stand for the 'one nation' which was dear to the old ruling estate, nor does the left represent a working class with its own cherished values and attitudes as the old Labour Party did. Mixtures of historical layers can exist side by side for a long time. It is quite likely that this will happen in Britain. But such geological faults of old and new cannot detract from the fact that change will take the country closer to other countries, who abandoned their feudal remnants much earlier.

Sam Brittan, in discussing trade unions, has described the position of people who take action in one capacity which they dislike in another. As unionists they help raise wages, but as consumers they resent the resulting increases in prices. Such confusions of interest have become almost general today.[2] What people want, depends very largely on situation and circumstance. The same individuals have different interest in different circumstances. This presupposes, of course, that individuals are no longer wholly members of one class or even estate. It means that they have become floating voters rather than status voters. Such individualisation implies that the values of the new middle classes play a greater part than before. The result is an uncertain society, not as close-knit as was the old British estate system, not as homely perhaps, but full of options and even of economic opportunities.

Is this desirable? What, in any case, about the values described in this section? Are they sources of delight or of dismay? It does not matter much, of course, whether one likes what happens or not; it will happen in any case. Thus it is more a nostalgic comment than a prescription to remark that I take no pleasure in watching the old balance of modernity and history go. It probably had to go; but nevertheless this is a pity. Nostalgia apart, there remains a real issue. Change is never total; even revolutions leave untouched important traditions of countries. The question is whether there is any way of saving at least some of the strengths of Britain's tradition while accepting the changes which are happening. Can one, in other words, turn these changes to best advantage? After all, human life chances are not just choices which we can make; choices have to have meaning, and such meaning is given by belonging and believing. There may have been too much of both in the non-industrial industrial world of Britain; but there is too little of them in the highly industrial world of Germany, or of America. It is therefore worth aiming at a new balance of tradition and progress.

What this means, is simple in theory, if difficult in practice. In the terms of these chapters it means a merger of old and new middle classes to which both contribute. More generally, strands of Britain's history would have to be woven into its present from its future. There is the value of solidarity, for example. Solidarity has held things together and thereby provided people with a social safety net which they badly need in a modern society. Solidarity can be divisive, as we have seen, but there is no reason why the beneficial force of this traditional attitude should not be preserved for the country as a whole as well as for its constituent parts, despite a greater emphasis on individual advancement and improvement. Economic success does not have to be as disruptive as in fact it has been in some European countries. Britain could not, and should not, imitate Japan; but there are elements in its history which would allow a comparable development.

This may be a pious wish. But the wish must be given rein, especially since it can build on realities. The trouble is of course that these realities are themselves under pressure. There is the official pressure from those who would prefer a society entirely determined by individual competition to one in which solidarity remains important, because productivity is uppermost in their minds. They fail to see that an agreement on wages, productivity and profits is likely to be more effective than the threat of unemployment. There is the opposing pressure of those who would prefer to see solidarity channelled into a class struggle for power. They fail to see that such a struggle has never yet made the combatants happier, or better off. Then there is the uglier pressure by those who want to exclude new groups from the band of solidarity. They will have to be overruled, even if this requires what Americans call 'affirmative action', that is, positive discrimination in favour of systematically disadvantaged minorities. Then there is simply the dissipation of society in the cities and elsewhere. More and more individuals fall through the ever wider meshes of the net of social cohesion. A deliberate effort is needed to make sure that the net does not tear, and indeed that its meshes, while possibly woven into a different pattern, become tighter again.

So, does class matter? The answer is clearly yes. Using the term in the loose way in which we have used it throughout, the layer-cake of Britain's class structure may have been a mixed blessing, but it was also a blessing. It failed to promote industrial progress. Its static character, and notably the fact that the industrial class settled down to its own position in it, did not help growth or productivity. But the same facts have held British society together. The upper class set the tone, the working class espoused most clearly the prevailing values of solidarity, and the middle class transformed the potential of civil war into the reality of self-discipline and peaceful cohesion. Today, bonds of class in this sense are weakening. New groups are coming to the fore which do not share the values of the traditional estates. This is inevitable. It means that the old status structure of Britain is crumbling. Perhaps it is even desirable. It means that a growing number of people are liberated for choices which their parents did not have. But the question remains whether it must also mean that the sense of solidarity and cohesion which went with the old structure is breaking up. One hopes that the answer can be no.

WESTMINSTER, AND
OTHER INSTITUTIONS

Chapter Ten
A PLACE OF STRIFE

It may not be class war, but surely the most visible expression of the resentment bred by fine distinctions has been provided for some time by strikes and other industrial disputes. These are in fact the original symptoms of the 'British disease'. It may be that the actual figures of days lost do not display Britain to disadvantage as much as an eyewitness would suspect; but both the number of disputes and the extent to which they have turned from fights between employers and unions to fights at the expense of the public are remarkable. The British public is notably long-suffering; there is always a car pool, or even a bicycle, if public transport is on strike, never mind the inconvenience. One can nevertheless understand the strong terms in which Charles Rowley, for example, describes the situation: 'The term "extortion" refers to . . . an act of obtaining payments for not imposing harmful effects on other citizens. In my view, it is by the use of such extortion that unionised labour has since 1973 subverted the political process from a minority position within the voting spectrum.'[1] Rowley's fault is that he places the blame for disputes squarely on the shoulders of the unions, when today many realise that the story is in fact rather more complicated.

For one thing, management plays its part in disputes. Management attitudes are frequently not only remote, but anxious or hostile. They thereby help generate disputes. The remoteness has to do with the social drawers in which people are put, and with fine distinctions. On being promoted to foreman, a worker has to leave his union; he is now one of 'them'. 'They', on the other hand, show their subordinates that they are in charge. It is not only the dining room and the car and the plush and distant office which marks the distinction of management, but above all the unreadiness to talk and explain. For many in Britain, managing seems to mean giving instructions, when in fact it is a permanent process of persuasion. If instructions are not followed, it is invariably the fault of those who should obey, rather than of those whose authoritarian style does not fit the times, or the situation.

The most important instrument of management detachment is information. At the same time, the most important prerequisite of effective labour-management co-operation is information. By withholding information, management may introduce into industrial relations a totally unnecessary element of secrecy. Secrecy breeds distrust. Before long, labour does not believe management even if it decides to disclose relevant information. There is an assumption that management has something up its sleeve, because it has so often behaved as if it did. The result is that labour knows no bounds for its demands and indeed for its destructive action. But when management begins to scream that the future of the enterprise itself is in jeopardy, nobody listens any more.

Attitudes to conflict are a crucial management skill. They are also determined by the culture in which one has been brought up and lives. There are countries in which managers quite naturally follow two main principles: one is that only the powerless have to fear losing face, so a dispute must not turn into a mutual worry about losing face; the other is that every effort has to be made to define the dispute in such a way that both sides can win. It may be, indeed it is likely, that one side wins more than the other; but it is quite unnecessary to engage in a fight in which all the gains are on one, and all the losses on the other, side. There are managers in Britain who follow these principles. But they are not the majority. The majority dislikes the other side intensely, would like them to lose, even appeals to government if they cannot win by themselves, and in any case fights tooth and nail for its own position.

Such attitudes are of course not confined to management. 'The other side' takes much the same view. This is all the more pronounced since the other side can by no means be identified with national union leaders. Rare is the case in which a British manager can mobilise his workers against their distant leaders in London. In fact, most national union leaders are led from behind when it comes to disputes. Characteristically, most disputes start 'unofficially', and are sanctioned by the union after the event. An anonymous industrialist has described the situation in an article entitled 'The Wonder That There Aren't Even

More Strikes'. He says that those who have argued, in recent years, that the power of national union leaders has passed to local shop stewards are wrong. 'Power has not passed to the shop stewards. They are usually elected annually by their men and are given practically no power of decision. If they don't do what the men want, they are sacked. I know, because I have seen it happen. Over and over again, I have talked and "communicated" with shop stewards, and won them over to more reasonable attitudes – only to meet new faces after the elections.'[2]

One wonders whether, by 'reasonable', the anonymous industrialist means his point of view, or something which might be described as a common interest. Also, the quotation and these comments must not be misread to imply that trade unions have no power. Their power is great, especially in the political process. But their power is not suspended in mid-air. It is based on a widespread propensity to assume antagonistic interests and to fight for one's own corner. Moreover, this view is shared by many members of the public. Peregrine Worsthorne describes facts of life when he observes that 'trade unions have a cause that excuses excess'; 'trade union violence ... enjoys a much wider degree of tolerance and provokes a much less absolutely hostile response' than any other kind of violence; 'trade unionists now enjoy a special dispensation, a unique exculpatory glamour that takes much of the sting out of public criticism'.[3] But the point behind these observations is that the public consists very largely of trade unionists, and that these trade unionists support union action.

There are three facts which impress one about industrial disputes in Britain, facts which have a wider significance.

First of all, there has of course been a great deal of public criticism of industrial disputes in general, and of trade unions in particular in recent years. At times, one suspects, such public criticism has led voters who are, as trade unionists, members of the Labour Party, to vote Conservative. On three occasions since the late 1960s, it has led governments to legislate 'in place of strife'. The first time, legislation was prevented at the last moment by extra-parliamentary pressure, notably by the unions. This was under Harold Wilson. The second time, legislation was enacted, but it turned out to be impossible to enforce it. This was under Edward Heath; the Act was repealed when Harold Wilson returned to power. The third time, an Employment Act was introduced which confined itself to curbing certain obvious excesses, such as 'secondary picketing', and left the core area of disputes and union activity alone. This was under Margaret Thatcher.

In many countries, this story would be regarded as scandalous. If a parliamentary majority wants to introduce a bill, or has enacted legislation, then the law of the land dominates all special interests. Not so in Britain. In Britain, industrial disputes are very largely governed by a legal taboo. Indeed, they have been declared taboo by successive legislation ever since the Trade Disputes Act of 1906. There is much behind this taboo which is characteristic of British attitudes and institutions. The law has no place in disputes between social and political groups. Cyril Grunfeld is clearly right when he sees in the definition of independent trade unions by the Appeal Tribunal an 'unspoken acceptance . . . of a conflict philosophy of industrial relations': 'An independent trade union might well be thought to be one which was capable of standing on its own feet in the sense that it was not only independent of an employer but able, if need be, to adopt as uncompromising an attitude towards an employer as might be necessary in any given circumstances.'[4] These are the words of a tribunal! Evidently, the law has opted out of industrial conflict. This means that there is an underlying view that such disputes should take their own course. Group conflict is, as it were, an autonomous social process, regulated only by its participants. The law on the other hand has its circumscribed sphere which does not extend either to industrial or to political conflict.

How do the participants regulate their conflict? There are numerous rules for collective bargaining, many of them re-negotiated as often as there are disputes. In some areas, there are procedures for arbitration and conciliation. But what does not exist, except in a small number of unusual enterprises, is a systematic attempt to create institutions of co-operation. This is the second point to be made about industrial conflict in Britain. The prevailing view is that there are irreconcilable conflicts of interest between employers and labour, and that it would be blurring the lines if an attempt was made to share responsibility and authority. Blurring the lines is regarded by both sides as not only inappropriate, but disadvantageous; it restricts the chances of management to give instructions, and the chances of labour to fight all-out battles.

This is not the view taken in most other countries. In Europe, some form of industrial democracy has been introduced in law or in fact almost everywhere. Workers, through their representatives, participate in the management of affairs at many levels of the enterprise. The system is probably most developed in Germany. Contrary to the impression given by many, it is not co-determination on supervisory boards that matters most. It matters, because it provides union leaders and a few other employee representatives with a regular flow of information, so that the British dialogue of the deaf is avoided. But supervisory boards are at a distance for most. The more important, and older, institution is that of 'works councils', in which elected representatives of the work-force who may or may not be union members, are not only informed of, but are involved in decisions, especially in the personnel field. Works councils were introduced in German industry in 1920, as a leftover of the otherwise shortlived *soviet*, or council movement. Today, they have become an effective thermometer of employee moods, but also an important corrective of management intentions.

By contrast, British industry has remained a place of strife. The prevailing view remains one of all-or-nothing battles. When a Committee of Enquiry on Industrial Democracy was established in 1976 under the chairmanship of Lord Bullock, and came up with proposals for institutional change in British industry, it was not only split, but found the trade unionists in an embarrassing position.[5] They signed, because they realised that others intended to make them a present of co-determination; but they were by no means unhappy when it turned out that the report soon sank without a trace. On the whole, union leaders would go out of their way to insist that they should not be involved in making decisions in individual firms. Management is management, and labour is labour; it is wrong to blur the lines. Everybody has a job to do, and nobody can do the job of the other. This is the kind of attitude which prevails.

It is only a step from this attitude to the third and most serious fact concerning British industrial disputes. Textbooks about industrial relations tell us that one limit of conflict is the survival of the enterprise itself. In Britain one wonders whether this is always the case. While management may wake up too late to argue the case for survival, labour at times does not stop short of destroying the viability of firms. Workers have in fact struck themselves out of their jobs. In the nationalised industries, this effect remains concealed, because the taxpayer has to shoulder the deficit; but the same attitude prevails. Conflicts can become a social ritual apparently unrelated to economic interests. It is continued almost for its own sake. And it is a win-or-lose conflict which can end only if one side has succeeded in making the other side budge.

For this is the underlying attitude which we are describing here: a win-or-lose attitude. In game theory, there is the expression, 'zero-sum' games. Zero-sum games are games in which one side loses what the other one gains. In British industry, a zero-sum attitude prevails. Thoughts of compromise are not very high in people's minds. One fights to win. This is coupled with the gentlemanly virtue of fairness. On the whole, one accepts defeat gracefully, though not without a glint in the eye which betrays the thought of the next battle. One will get one's own back. In the meantime, the issue is one of winning or losing. The management attitude described earlier as being desirable could be called one of trying to convert zero-sum into positive-sum games, that is, redefining them in such a way that both sides can win a little. In Britain, however, many conflicts have in fact become negative-sum games, in which the only question is how one manages to minimise one's losses. Perhaps if one plays zero-sum games long enough, in industry at any rate all disputes become negative-sum games.

The zero-sum mentality is by no means confined to industry. It pervades human relations everywhere and dominates people's behaviour. It is as if social life were a cup game, an event in which one side has to win, even if this takes two replays and in the end even penalty kicks to decide. One is struck by different national reactions to sportsmen who, in events which are not cup games as such, say, athletics, do not come first. 'Silver medal for Germany', German papers would proudly announce if it was Wessinghage, whereas in British papers one would be more likely to find the headline, 'Ovett beaten', if he had come second. When the British are called sportsmanlike, this is what people mean. It is the love of a fight, the desire to win, coupled with the readiness to accept defeat graciously. What is missing (at least in more serious contests than those of sports) is recognition of the need for one's opponent to save face and get at least something, and that the battle itself can contribute to improvements for all.

This approach to conflict tallies, of course, with the static structure of class. If there is no movement in the layers, no one group which wants to change its position within the whole, then conflicts are a kind of ritual. They are enacted, not without feeling, but under rules which are as generally accepted as the layer-cake itself. They repeat themselves at regular intervals. But they do not change what one might well call 'the system', nor are they intended to do so. Conflicts are a part of life, and so what matters is to make them as bearable as possible. What better model for this than that of sports! Zero-sum games are fun, like so many things British, but more often than not they are distinctly unhelpful.

Before this analysis is applied to the heartland of British disputes, to Westminster, one footnote is necessary. The picture drawn in this chapter is once again a generalisation, and it neglects recent changes. There are managers and unionists to whom, indeed there are many firms in which, at least some of the generalisations offered here do not apply. The very fact that legislation is not regarded as an appropriate instrument of conflict regulation, encourages individual enterprises to try and find ways of creating more permanent structures of industrial democracy. The fact that it is variegated and unconstrained by the law may well be regarded as a source of strength in British industry, so far as coming to terms with differences of interest is concerned.

The picture drawn here is also more historical than contemporary. Historians may well conclude that the 1979 election marks a watershed for trade unions. Not only have the inner councils of the Labour Party, and of the unions themselves, decided that the 'winter of discontent' in 1978–79 lost Labour the election; it has also become clear that large numbers of workers have deserted Labour. They may not have done so for good. The crucial point is the ambiguity in people's class position. As Sam Brittan put this plausibly: more and more often, 'the end result of action taken by people through collective activity will be unacceptable to the same people in their capacity of consumers and voters – a perverse invisible hand'.[6] In other words, the trade unionist and the consumer fight each other within the same soul. Sometimes one wins, sometimes the other; but in any case support for the unions is no longer absolute. Dare one hope that this marks the beginning of a new phase of industrial relations in which, to follow a proposal by Keith Middlemas,[7] self-regulation rather than legislation restrains the combatants?

Chapter Eleven
THE WESTMINSTER GAME

The seating plan of the House of Commons is highly significant. Two sets of benches are facing each other, one for the Government, one for the Opposition. There are no cross-benches, as in the House of Lords which in this respect as in others, is so much more civilised. There certainly is no semi-circle as in most other parliaments, which allows visual expression for many shades of opinion. The House of Commons has no centre. It has a Speaker who presides in the way which is characteristic of British life. Whoever wants to speak, has to 'catch his eye'; there is no entitlement, and certainly no 'speakers' list'. Both sides have their generals in front, on the front benches, where they sit facing each other. In some Commonwealth parliaments, which have imitated the Westminster model but which are much smaller, Prime Minister and leader of the opposition are so close to each other that they could almost hit each other over the head with the volumes of legal texts between them. However, not so long ago a leading member of one of the British parties gripped the mace, crossed the floor, and threatened to hit an adversary over the head with it.

The story which the seating plan of the House of Commons illustrates is that of adversary politics. The notion has been developed by Samuel Finer, who is therefore best qualified to explain it. 'Briefly, the adversary system is a stand-up fight between two adversaries for the favour of the lookers-on. . . Since 1945 especially, our public life has been conducted in [this] way, with two rival teams in open contention which goes on before an election, during an election, and – above all – continues after the election, in the form of continuous polemic across the floor of the Commons where a powerless Opposition confronts an all-powerful Government, in the hope of winning itself a more favourable verdict at the next general election.'[1] Finer makes much of the asymmetry of the fight. In fact, Government as a rule has an almost unbeatable position. Its legislation is certain of passage; it enjoys large-scale personal patronage; it has a monopoly of information and research assistance. Its only weakness is in fact the possibility of losing the next election. 'Governments enjoying this plenitude of power, patronage and information do, however, alternate with one another. Our system is one of alternating single-party government.'[2]

Sam Finer clearly does not like this system very much. His arguments will be examined in due course. Yet there is a case for the system. It may not be the one that was made when it evolved (naturally, it was not created by an act of constitutional parthenogenesis); but this does not make it any the weaker. The case is, in a word, one for clear lines of conflict. There are different interests, and one may as well have the differences out. The only way to do this, and not to sweep them under the carpet, is by giving one side the chance to do what it thinks is right, while letting the other expose in debate the weaknesses of this side and canvass the support of the electorate for its views. If the opposite of the adversary system is the consensus system, it is certainly true that in such a system differences rarely emerge clearly. More often than not they are expressed in smoke-filled rooms. Politics is about agreement, not about confrontation. As a result, all clear-cut interests are submerged in a sugar fluff of compromise.

Politics in the Federal Republic of Germany follows very nearly the opposite principle to that of British politics. Four facts make the case. Most governments since 1948 have been coalition governments. (In Britain, there has not been a coalition government since the war, unless one wants to count the short period of a parliamentary Lib-Lab pact in 1977–78; indeed, adversary politics is supposed to prevent coalition.) Parliament in Germany works through a system of committees which may be chaired by a member of the opposition, and which in any case show much continuity of membership and attitudes. (In Britain, Select Committees for most departments of government are a recent innovation; and their status is such that what they say can easily be discounted by Government.) There is, in Germany, a second chamber composed of representatives of the *Länder*, the states, which can block legislation, in which case a 'conciliation committee' has to work out an acceptable compromise. (In Britain, government is all but unicameral; the House of Lords has no real blocking power, in part because it does not have a constituency; in any case there are no states in the British system.) In Germany, all legislation is subject to review by the courts, and notably the constitutional court; indeed the possible views of the courts influence the legislative process at every stage. (In Britain, of course, there is neither a constitution nor a constitutional court; as we have seen, the role of the judiciary in politics is minimal.)

The difference between the electoral systems of the two countries is thus no accident. In Germany, only half the members of parliament are constituency members in the British sense; the other half are elected on party lists. In this way, a high degree of proportional representation is achieved. The British electoral system is neither as old as is sometimes implied nor was it always as clear-cut as it has been since the abolition of university seats. It is only after the war that it has become a true single-member system. Since then, however, the first-past-the-post electoral system has operated throughout the country. It has meant that every constituency had one and only one member, and that he or she was the one who had got a relative majority of votes.

This is where the critics of the adversary system begin their onslaught. The electoral system makes for unfair representation and exaggerates differences. Sam Finer produces an impressive example from the 1920s. In 1922, Conservatives had 38.2 per cent of the vote, Liberals 29.1 per cent, and Labour 30.5 per cent. Yet, due to the plurality system in constituencies, the Tories had 346 seats, and Labour, with more than three-quarters the Tory vote, only 142; indeed Labour and Liberals together, with 60 per cent of the votes, had only 40 per cent of the seats. Worse still, a year later, the three parties had almost the same percentages of the vote (38.1–29.6–30.5). Yet by the flukes of the electoral system, the Conservatives had lost nearly a hundred seats, whereas Liberals and Labour had each gained nearly 50. It is indeed hard to see fairness in such shifts. Since the war, there have been changes of government in 1945, 1951, 1964, 1970, 1974, and 1979. At times, the governing party had a plurality of more than 100 seats. Yet at no time did any party achieve 50 per cent of the popular vote. This is how the electoral system exaggerates changes in party affiliation and supports the adversary system.

A more serious point has to do with the kind of political party, and the quality of party competition which is produced by the system. The adversary principle and the electoral system tend to force parties away from the centre. The system places a premium on extremism, or at any rate, on the undiluted representation of clear-cut, but non-moderate interests. This has been particularly pronounced since 1974, though it was present before. For the electorate, this undoubtedly means a clear choice rather than one between virtually indistinguishable alternatives. But does the electorate want such a choice? In fact, the voters do not share the extremism of political parties. To quote Sam Finer again: 'This off-centre policy of one or the other of the two parties has never been supported by a majority of the electorate . . . The electorate's views are more stable and more centrist; but such tiny swings and ripples as appear among it are distorted into large parliamentary majorities, and hence, given the unrepresentative partisanship of parliamentary parties, to wide swings in policy.'[3]

These swings in policy, and the uncertainty attendant on them, are indeed the most forceful argument against adversary politics. Sam Finer reproduces the infamous list of policies which have been changed at least once from one extreme to the other since the war, and over which there is therefore very little certainty in people's minds: steel nationalisation; taxation of wealth and high incomes; rent regulation; economic planning; land development; trade union privileges; comprehensive schools. Perhaps economic planning sits a little awkwardly in this list. It is much more general than the rest. Indeed, what Tom Wilson calls 'the economic cost of the adversary system' requires a special comment in the next chapter. 'The difficulties of stabilisation, already formidable enough, were enhanced by the possibility that small swings of votes at the frequent elections would lead to a change of Government.'[4]

It would be facile to heap further abuse on the British political system. The parties which are the protagonists of the great battle, for example, are themselves hardly democratic. One is dominated by a ruling clique and is in many ways merely a support machine for this clique; the other is dominated by a clique which has power, though it does not rule. There is no Political Parties Act which regulates internal party democracy, or even the method of choosing candidates, nor is there likely to be such an act. There are, of course, more than two parties. Indeed, the 1974–79 parliament was clearly a multi-party parliament with first a shaky, then a non-existent majority. The Liberals have consistently done well in elections in the 1970s; yet their representation is miniscule by comparison. In 1974, they polled 18.3 per cent of the vote, but in the end got no more than 13 seats. Under proportional representation, they would have had 116 seats. Regional parties with a vote concentrated in a small number of constituencies do better under the British system. Thus, Scottish and Welsh Nationalists had eleven and three seats respectively in the 1974 Parliament. Including the various Northern Irish groups there were, in fact, eight, and, at the time of the dissolution of Parliament in 1979, twelve, political parties in all. Despite their electoral support, however, the 'minor' parties were only occasionally a part of the contest.

But enough of this tale of woe. What has happened to the political system which was the envy of the world? Did not Westminster stand for everything that was desirable in a democracy? Many countries have borrowed their parliamentary institutions from Westminster, Speaker's wig and all. Others, like the German *Bundestag*, have often discussed the question of how they could liven up their rather stolid proceedings by importing procedures from Westminster. As a result, to give but one example, question time was introduced. The House of Commons certainly is lively. It is the place where every issue of any significance is likely to be raised, as well as one where every view, however insignificant, is expressed. There is a sense in which despite its apparent unrepresentative character, Parliament is a mirror of the nation. It reflects not only interests and views, but also moods and concerns. It is an enviable institution.

There is at least one much more serious reason why this should be so. It has to do with change. Democracy is after all about change. Its greatest strength is that it allows change without revolution. It is an institutional mechanism which makes it possible for new interests to come to the fore without the representatives of the old ones being hanged or imprisoned. One need hardly be reminded today that this is anything but a matter of course. The fact that a change of government has come about at least six times since the war, speaks well for the system. In this sense, Westminster still is democracy at work.

Nor must one merely contrast this system with dictatorships. Dictatorship is by no means the only alternative to the Westminster game. There are democracies which find change exceedingly difficult. At least one of the great democracies of the world, Japan, has not had a change of government since the war. Is it absurd to assume that such stability must lead to stagnation which in turn must generate violent demands for change, or at least demonstrations of protest? Stagnation is, of course, possible even in democracies which have seen changes in government. The problem of the German system is that its institutions are too strongly bent on consensus. To be sure, every now and again there are changes in government policy which are contested by the opposition. The great debate on Willy Brandt's *Ostpolitik* is probably the supreme example during the 1970s, though Adenauer's *Westpolitik* in the 1950s could also be cited. But in domestic matters, controversy has all but died down. Beneath a noisy surface of polemic there is widespread agreement. Moreover, the agreement nowadays extends to foreign policy as well. Legal restraints define the area of political division closely. The way in which parliament, government and bureaucracy are intertwined assures a widespread consensus. Where this is not achieved the first time round, the second chamber will see to it. The main political parties all fight for the centre. As a consequence, the centre is crowded, if not overcrowded, and the extremes are ignored. Stability turns into immobility, or at any rate into a great institutional reluctance to accept change. The extremes find expression outside the parliamentary system and are forced to threaten the system itself. One does not want to extrapolate from this situation if one is German and loves freedom. But in this respect at least the evidence indicates that the Westminster game has its advantages.

Chapter Twelve
SHORT-TERM THINKING

The Westminster game is not only adversary, it is also amusing. This is due to no small extent to the fact that it is topical. It does not take long for a newspaper revelation to be translated into a parliamentary question; and when a matter is discussed by Parliament, it grips public opinion entirely. At any rate it grips those who allow their time scales to be dominated by Westminster. Once, a group of parliamentary lobby correspondents asked me whether I could help them find out about experiences with federalism. When I recommended a seminar in a few months' time, they were rather taken aback. Oh no! they needed to know by Monday week. They did not say so, but they might have added that after Monday week they would no longer be interested. And even today it would be possible to identify the week in 1979 in which the lobby correspondents asked for advice.

Short-term thinking is a popular British pastime. It may or may not have its origin in Parliament; but Parliament certainly demonstrates it to the full. The rim of the saucer beyond which the House of Commons looks, is rarely even the next election, rather the next budget. Since recent governments have taken to introducing more than one budget a year, this is a very short time-scale indeed. It is made all the more striking by another recent innovation, that is, governments making U-turns and thereby turning into their own adversaries. All this does not hold for the House of Lords. Indeed, the second chamber has many virtues as well as evident weaknesses. One day, one may well wish to build on these virtues. But for the moment, it clearly stands in the shadow of the House of Commons, which is as it should be.

On several occasions, reference has been made to life and institutions in Britain being fun, amusing, interesting, enjoyable. Such aesthetic categories are hardly appropriate for assessing political institutions, or class, for that matter. Yet they are unavoidable. It is true that parliamentary life in Germany, and by no means only in Germany, is not fundamentally different from that of a bureaucracy. Even its high points are contrived. Most of the time, it requires above all patience, and what Germans call with an untranslatable word, *Sitzfleisch*. This has to do with the flesh on which we sit, which has to be well developed in a bureaucratised world. By contrast, a British MP has more need for his feet and his mouth. Many nights, he leaves a dinner party at 9.30 pm to go and vote, not by raising his hand but by walking into a division lobby. Many weekends he travels to his constituency to hold a surgery. Much of the time, he stands in the bar of the Commons talking to others. And he talks, talks, talks. All this is true as well for her, the woman MP, of course. It is a unique, perhaps frustrating, but rapidly moving and eventful life. The life of the MP might well stand for the nature of Britain's political process, and not just for politics alone.

But there is a price. It would be vain to deny it. Some might be prepared to pay the price; indeed they might not regard it as a price at all. Others are concerned. We have already quoted Tim Wilson on the economic cost of the adversary system which is also the cost of short-term thinking. Wilson points to the difficulties of stabilisation arising from changes in government. He adds at that point that the party in power might be tempted 'to take risks on the eve of an election which it might well have avoided if its position had been more secure and the needs of stabilisation had therefore been more soberly assessed'.[1] However, temptation is by no means confined to the eve of an election. It could be argued that several recent governments have spent years trying to undo the damage which resulted from their first budget. In general, the volatility of the political process does not help when it comes to stabilising economic development, and instilling confidence in investors. If the rim of the saucer of political thinking is so close that one almost forgets the saucer, the condition in which one is, then this is bound to spill over into the economic process. Short-term thinking is infectious.

Indeed, there are signs that the financial institutions have borrowed some of the practices of politics. They are, of course, directly affected by budgets, and by the Treasury in general. It is therefore not surprising that they should adopt the time scale of Parliament. It is nevertheless damaging. In 1980, Harold Lever and George Edwards published a series of articles on Britain's banks which led to a lively, polemical, and inconclusive debate.[2] Lever and Edwards argued that one of the main weaknesses of Britain's industry was the absence of long-term loans, and of the kind of commitment of financial institutions to industry which is characteristic of Japan, or of Germany. They castigated the interest of banks in the immediate and short-term. The banks responded by pointing out that the charge is incorrect. They produced evidence of long-term investment and long-term credit by the clearing banks and other financial institutions. They also showed that they take an interest in industry by employing experts, giving advice at the local level, etcetera.

The evidence of the banks is incontrovertible. Moreover, it is always dubious to start an assault on a complicated system at one end and ignore avenues of equal or greater importance. The banks behave as British banks, and no one can be surprised by that. Indeed, there is evidence that foreign banks in London, like Japanese managers in Wales, have adopted different practices. They do not observe the fine distinction between banker and borrower which prevents many British bankers from asking their borrowers awkward questions. Foreign banks ask many awkward questions, and as a result they can take the likely prospects of a firm as a satisfactory collateral rather than insisting on assets. Moreover, insofar as British banks have changed, it is characteristic that all these changes are recent. Indeed, the banks go out of their way to point out that it is only a few years since they have modified their practices. The tradition, then, is one of static and short-term lending.

The banks share this tradition, to be sure, with their borrowers. In a world of gentlemen, the borrowers did not want to disclose information about the quality of their staff, or 'secret' new plans in production and marketing. They preferred to risk their assets. Moreover, directors of companies are all set to make quick profits. The notion of a firm providing employment and producing output, but not making profit, for many years, while it gradually finds its niche in the market, is not very widespread in Britain. Still less are directors and bankers inclined to support an enterprise through a trough, help restructure it, appoint new management, discuss possible new products, and explore new markets together. The story of AEG-Telefunken in Germany, where all this happened with the help of the Dresdner Bank, is not yet complete. The venture may yet fail. But even to try it without calling for the assistance of government shows a different attitude by all concerned.

Britain has the most efficient, adaptable, and experienced financial institutions in the world. The City is an enormous asset to the country. It is an industry in its own right which employs 360,000 people, and earns a sizeable portion of national income.[3] It is also a switchboard of international trade, the like of which not even New York, let alone Hong Kong, Zurich, or Frankfurt, to say nothing of Luxemburg, has been able to create. But the international versatility of the City was, until recently at least, not matched by its interest in domestic industry. Moreover, the efficiency of the City rests on its ability to provide returns. London's preoccupation is one for returns rather than for maintaining capital. Still less is the City concerned with sustaining British industry. Once again, it is evident how closely weakness and strength are related.

There are ways of mitigating the weakness of short-term thinking. The House of Lords has already been mentioned. Of the civil service more will have to be said. One way which has proved effective elsewhere is to remind decision-makers regularly of longer-term perspectives by putting day-to-day decisions in context. There are a variety of methods for doing this. In Germany, there is a statutory Council of Economic Advisors (*Sachverständigenrat*) which reports annually on the state of the economy and the needs of economic policy. The French *Commissariat au Plan* has been transformed, in recent years, from a planning agency to one which accompanies government policy with analysis and advice. Perhaps this was intended by the creation of the government 'think tank', the Central Policy Review staff, under the Heath government. It was indeed undoubtedly the case, as long as Lord Rothschild was in charge. Since then, a number of reports, some more, some less controversial, have been produced. But these reports were already related to declared government intentions. In principle, they could have been produced by the civil service. I was therefore not surprised when I heard someone say about the Central Policy Review staff that it would be worth relinquishing one research assistant for every ten feet one came closer to No. 10 Downing Street.

The American way of achieving the same end is, not surprisingly, based on private initiative. The Brookings Institution in Washington began by analysing the federal budget, which had not until then been done by the Treasury Department. Nowadays, the Brookings Institution is out of favour with government as being too far to the left.

Whereas in the past, members of the Brookings Institution moved easily into and out of government, this privilege has now passed to a number of other institutions, such as the Georgetown Center for Strategic and International Studies, the Wilson Center, and the American Enterprise Institute. But these too are places where the medium term dominates. They do not share the academic time-scales which are essentially indefinite, and have to be such because to seek to know the causes of things is an open-ended intention. They do not accept the political time-scales either, because they are too short everywhere. Thus, they attract straddlers, people who live easily both in the academic and in the political world. They produce reports which are, to use a horrible but apposite word, relevant. Above all, they listen and are listened to, and are thereby able to add the dimension of continuity to an intrinsically discontinuous process.

Attempts to create a similar institution in Britain have so far failed. I was myself involved in these attempts, so that I am aware of the problem. There are of course research centres with a public-policy intent. There is above all the Policy Studies Institute which has resulted from a merger of PEP ('Political and Economic Planning'), which was founded in 1931, and the Centre for Studies in Social Policy. But there is not only a shortage of competition; there is also an absence of relevance. London, with all its variegated and splendid institutions, has so far not been able to create a centre where those who take time to think and those who are involved in decisions meet and inspire each other. In this respect, too, it has failed to extend the rim of the saucer. So far, the Westminster game has succeeded in dominating even public-policy research and thought.

Chapter Thirteen
A CORPORATE BIAS

Before going further, it had better be stated firmly and clearly that the Westminster game is only a part of the British political process. Sam Finer points out one of the reasons for this fact, though he is then distracted by his polemic against adversary politics. He describes in vivid terms the preponderance of government in the British system. It is well to remember: power, patronage and information are all the government's. What happens in Westminster is, from the government's point of view, little more than a nuisance, even a waste of time. One has to go and answer questions, or make cases for bills which one knows perfectly well will be enacted. Ministers often regard this as all but useless. They prefer to concentrate on the difficult business of governing.

The business of governing, on the other hand, is anything but adversary. Harold Rose is the political scientist who has stressed this against Samuel Finer and others.[1] In government, there is much continuity. For one thing, there is the civil service. The civil service is a *service*, not a political actor. Nevertheless, its command of facts and arguments, and its continuity of service, makes it a strong force for consensus. Sir Antony Part put his experience as a Permanent Secretary into words when he said in a television programme that the civil service always tries to nudge governments to the centre. This may or may not be done for reasons of the political convictions of civil servants. (What irony that civil servants should be closer in their politics to the majority of the electorate than any political party!) It is probably inevitable. Even countries which have replaced the independent civil service by a political service have found that it happens. Since in the medium term, that is after at most two years, no government can govern against the civil service, or to put it more controversially, every government is captured by its civil service, there tends to be much more continuity to the Westminster game than strikes the eye of the onlooker.

Continuity however is by no means merely a sinister result of the influence of unaccountable civil servants. It is in the nature of any modern industrial society that there should be a tendency to bring about agreement on certain crucial issues. This is particularly true for the core area of economic policy, that is, the relationship between government, trade unions and employers. Keith Middlemas has traced the history of this relationship in Britain since 1911, in his book, *Politics in Industrial Society*. His main argument is that since the First World War, and strongly influenced by the national consensus of the two wars, there has been a growing tendency to establish 'a new form of harmony in the political system'.[2] This was not an easy process; it has its ups and downs. The General Strike was certainly an event which strained the achievements of the years 1916–25 to breaking point. But the process continued, as a 'journey to the centre, 1923–31', as a time of 'compromise and harmony, 1931–39', as a reaction to 'emergency, 1935–40', then as a war-time coalition, and after the Second World War in the ways which came to be represented most clearly by the author of *The Middle Way*, Harold Macmillan.

The essence of this process, as Middlemas sees it, is consensus on the basic data of the economic process, and on social policy. Time and again, there came to be an explicit or unspoken concordat between the 'corporate triangle' of government, unions and employers. This started with 'Lloyd George's contract' which led to the emergence of powerful institutions on both sides of industry and involved the abandonment of revolutionary ambitions by working-class organisations; and·it ended with the 'social contract' of Harold Wilson and Jack Jones, though that may already be another matter. Critics of such developments have used the terms 'corporate state' for all concordats of this kind; but Keith Middlemas is more careful. 'The corporate triangle between government, employers and unions was not a system, as the corporate theorists of the thirties defined systems, but a tendency, or bias, central to the evolution of modern government. So highly was equilibrium valued by its partners that all, even government, abrogated large parts of their autonomy to preserve it. Institutions which had grown up in this form, largely at the will of governments, in turn came to depend on the state, and the state found itself dependent on the compromises thereby achieved. The capacity of political parties in government to alter direction was thus steadily reduced, until in many of the most vital questions of policy they could do no more than avoid crises – even in the emergency preceding the Second World War.'[3]

This is a powerful statement, and one which sounds very different from Finer's description of the adversary system. It is also a statement which makes one no less worried, albeit for different reasons. The corporate bias of Middlemas sounds much like German consensus politics, except that it takes place outside the orbit of visible political institutions. The consensus is secret, as it were. Westminster has almost nothing to do with it. Before we pursue this suspicion, it is as well to point out that what Middlemas calls the corporate bias has had at least some results which are by no means negligible, or negative. The most important is probably the extension of citizenship rights. It is T. H. Marshall's notion, in his *Citizenship and Social Class*, that general rights of citizenship have been extended from the legal through the political to the social sphere, and have thereby reduced the importance of social class. This is not the result of adversary politics. Citizenship has become part of the rules of the game which are removed from the battle. The extension of citizenship rights is thus both a part of an overriding contract, and the result of a contract. This contract is the political expression of the alliance between the classes which was characteristic of the two world wars.

Middlemas does not confine himself to describing the emergence and functioning of the corporate bias; he also argues that this great force for stability and progress has in fact declined. Somewhat surprisingly in view of Harold Wilson's 'social contract', he says that the new harmony 'lasted at least until the mid-sixties when the much-vaunted "consensus" was seriously, if not fatally, disrupted'.[5] Consensus came to mean inflexibility, bureaucratisation, unnecessary secrecy, uncontrolled power by unaccountable bodies. 'In a very general way, the supposed benefits of consensus came to be seen, not as high aspirations as in 1940, but as the lowest common denominator of policies designed to avoid trouble.'[6] As a result, the parties themselves began to 'destabilise, apparently deliberately' the system of corporate bias.[7] Both Labour and Conservatives sought alternative philosophies of society, such as the decentralised 'genuine democracy' of Tony Benn or Sir Keith Joseph's Friedmanite competition. While the arteries of the system hardened further, those responsible for setting it up turned away.

All this adds up to a complicated and somewhat confusing picture of British politics. It is time to take stock, therefore, and try to make sense of what has been said. In doing so, both Finer's and Middlemas's theories must be weighed carefully, without following either to the extremes to which their authors take them.

All modern societies have to try and bring about some degree of agreement between government, employers and labour; Britain is no exception. Characteristically, this need was most strongly felt during the wars, that is, when a national effort was required. But it did not end there. The relationship between wages, profits, productivity, growth, and government policies changes over time; but at all times the attempt to define it in ways which are plausible to the participants in the economy is important. Defining the problem does not mean signing and sealing a contract. At any rate it need not mean that. A common definition of economic parameters may well be largely implicit. Moreover, such agreements are bound to break down. But no such doubt can detract from the necessity to try and try again. Thus, it is not surprising that the three constituents of the corporate triangle tried to find common ground in Britain.

One of the consequences of this process has been to give the trade unions political power. It has been argued that the emergence of the Trade Union Congress was the condition and result of 'Lloyd George's contract'. Whatever the new umbrella organisation of the unions may have lacked in power with respect to shop stewards and the shop floor, it gained generously as compensation by access to the corridors of political power, including the most important corridor of all, that between the Cabinet Office in Whitehall and No 10 Downing Street. Unions had to be talked to even if they did not agree to a formal contract. On the employers' side the question of organisation was more difficult. The Confederation of British Industry never acquired the formal power which the TUC has had for some time. But then, employers always had prominent spokesmen. In any case, they were fewer and therefore easier to reach and to hear. Government, throughout this century and more particularly since 1914, spent much of its time on the triangular relationship which documented the prevailing corporate bias.

But the corporate bias was just that; it was in fact never a complete system. Indeed, it was always disrupted by shifts in policy arising from the adversary mood of the parties and of Parliament. Not only did one side of the House of Commons prefer one corner of the triangle, and the other side the other corner, but their whole attitude to the new harmony differed. For example, Labour had a natural tendency to try and control prices, whereas Conservatives were more concerned about holding down wages. This, at any rate, was so before the 'social contract' was agreed in 1974, and more particularly before James Callaghan came to No. 10 in 1976. Thus, it can be said that the adversary bias of official politics kept on interfering with the corporate bias of real politics, with the result that neither of them was allowed full play.

This is not said lightly. It has consequences which are serious and which have contributed to the weaknesses both of Britain's economy and polity. For one thing, it has to be understood that in important respects the Westminster game was, and is, a *game*. It would be going too far to say that it is not serious. It is certainly taken seriously by its players. Moreover, its adversary character has an influence on what happens. But what happens is not decided in Westminster. It is not even discussed at Westminster in any detail. As a result, the visible political game becomes strangely superficial. Parliament with its comet's tail of helpers and lobby correspondents and spectators is but a deceptively lively adversary surface of an increasingly arteriosclerotic corporate reality.

This corporate reality, on the other hand, has rarely been allowed to generate its full usefulness. Again, the economic effects of politics are the most important. In countries in which there is a reliable agreement of all concerned on what is reasonable in terms of wages and prices, what productivity and what profit needs there are, there is usually no shortage of investment. In Britain, this reliable agreement has time and again been upset by the effects of adversary relations. A new tax, or the massive reduction of an old one, new measures of nationalisation or of privatisation, and the like, have turned important elements of the economy into political footballs. The result has invariably been that investors wanted their profits quickly. What was lacking was that most precious of all commodities of economic policy, confidence. Confidence requires longer-term certainty, and such certainty was lacking in view of the interference of the adversary with the corporate bias.

Thus there is a sense in which Britain managed to have, at least since the First World War, the worst of both worlds – neither a real adversary, nor a real corporate system, but incomplete elements of both. This sounds worse than real developments were; but it indicates one of their great weaknesses. More importantly, however, Middlemas is probably right that the traditional corporate-adversary system is under pressure today. There is a widespread feeling that both sides of the equation have failed the country. At one and the same time, the curbing of the power of the corporate triangle and the strengthening of the political centre in the party game are both required. Social Democrats and Liberals make both demands, and neither of the other parties defends the traditional system. Once again, change will happen because it is happening already. Once again, the direction of change is uncertain.

Chapter Fourteen

LONDON AND THE REST

'Anybody who has to teach foreigners the basic elements of the working constitution of this country will dwell on four main points: the unitary nature of the State, the sovereignty of Parliament, the collective responsibility of the Cabinet for policy decisions, and – fuelling all these and providing they are dynamic – the two-party system.'[1] I thought it was better to quote Professor Finer on such basics since I am a foreigner who is, if not teaching the British, then discussing their affairs. Moreover, this is not a textbook in political science; its function is not to be systematic but to highlight a few facts and processes which help explain the British condition. There is no need, for example, to discuss the collective responsibility of the Cabinet for policy decisions. But Finer's list of basics contains one feature which cannot remain unmentioned, the unitary nature of the state. To put it more crudely, Britain is extraordinarily centralised, and worse, quite unwilling to accept the need for decentralisation.

Among the many fictions surrounding Britain's working constitution, the most important is that of the sovereignty of Westminster. Fiction is perhaps too harsh a word for a pleasing aura of beliefs which surrounds Parliament in particular. The sovereignty of Westminster means that all strands of power end in Parliament. Parliament has all the power, and only Parliament has the power. It can depose not only governments, but judges as well. It can make, suspend and annul laws. It can deal with the smallest and the biggest issues of state; indeed, by dealing with any issue, it turns it into one of state. No one must detract from this power of Parliament. Internationally, the sovereignty of the country through Parliament should be absolute. Domestically, no authority should exist which is not subject to the decisions of Parliament.

To be sure, this is not how the world works. The debate about Britain joining the European Community was as anachronistic as that about devolution. In fact, if not in theory, Parliament has long come to share its sovereignty with many others: other countries and international organisations, other constituents of the corporate triangle, local authorities and numerous 'quangos' as well as 'ngos' and 'gos', that is, non-governmental and governmental organisations. In other respects, such as dismissing judges, Parliament would be very chary of using its powers. Yet when all is said and done, there remains the fact that many strands do converge, if not in Westminster then in Whitehall. One may well add a number of other London addresses to the list: Smith Square with its party headquarters (although the Labour Party has now moved, and others never went there); the Bank of England and the City in general; the Inns of Court and the Law Courts; Buckingham Palace of course. Britain is a highly centralised country, not just a unitary state, but one that is run from London in virtually all respects.

As well it might be; for London is a most remarkable place. By that is not meant the London in which people live. In fact, Londoners, like inhabitants of the other large metropolitan centres of the world, actually do not live in London. They live in one of its numerous villages, in Brixton and Islington and the East End and Chelsea, and of course in Croydon and Richmond and Highgate. What is meant here is London as the world's greatest producer of abstractions. Abstractions? Well, most of the things produced in London are in fact not things, but paper. The abstractions on paper are of course not academic abstractions, inconsequential except for other academics. They are insurance policies and shares and legal opinions and administrative orders and manifestos, and reports, reports, reports. London breathes in millions of people every morning, including a few from its constituent villages, who produce this paper, and whom the town breathes out again in the evening to go back to their suburban or country homes.

London, the producer of consequential paper, does not sound very attractive. But London is attractive. For one thing, there is no other place in the world which combines Westminster and Whitehall, the City, the Law Courts, the professional institutions, a great university, a vast shopping district, and Covent Garden and the National Theatre and the British Museum and the National Gallery, as well as many other institutions, almost within a square mile. London is infinite possibilities. Most of them remain unused by any one person of course. The stockbroker who comes into Cannon Street each morning is not likely to be on the bus from Maidstone which crawls up the Old Kent Road at night to take its passengers to see 'No Sex Please, We're British', though quite a few politicians who have a small flat around Smith Square are also members of an Inn of Court, and millions are vaguely aware of the overwhelming plenitude of options which the city offers. Like other big cities it is noisy and dirty; nothing seems to work properly, indeed it is a miracle that anything works; but unlike other cities it really has everything.

Or is there anything that London does not offer? No doubt one can think of things. Despite the parks, the country is some way away.

London is not England, though it may be Britain which, after all, is itself an abstraction. But London stands very much in the way of Britain falling naturally into its constituent parts. One of the reasons why devolution is so difficult in Britain, is that a quarter of the British live in London and its *banlieue*, say, within twenty-five miles of Trafalgar Square. Scotland, yes; Wales, perhaps; but otherwise it is difficult to see how a federal Britain should be structured. It is almost impossible to conceive of a federal England south of Lancashire and Yorkshire, if this is not too objectionable a statement for the people of the West Country. This is surely one of the reasons why the first deliberate attempt to bring about devolution failed miserably in 1979. Giving devolved rights, including parliaments, just to Scotland and Wales is almost like separatism. At best creates autonomous regions in the Italian sense, like Sicily, and South Tyrol, or Alto Adige as the Italians like to call it.

Nevertheless, it would be surprising if the devolution debate was really dead. Not only is it tempting for impotent minorities to use the issue in order to gain influence. There is a certain vague sympathy, mixed with fear, among the majority. This is true even in Ireland, North and South. And the mixture of sympathy and fear produces passive tolerance. People do not actively object to Scottish or Welsh Nationalists. As a result, they can have their way to a considerable extent. This, moreover, corresponds with the trend of the times. After all, even Switzerland had years of violence in a French-speaking part of the canton of Berne, until in the end regional and national referenda led to the decision to set up a new canton of Jura in 1979; and at this very moment, this canton is fighting for the incorporation of a few villages which still belong in Berne. For many people small is beautiful. They want to know where they belong in a vast and anonymous world; and belonging to Britain, being run by a distant Westminster, is not good enough.

Federalism has obvious advantages, aside from the fact that it satisfies people's wish for a circumscribed unit to which they belong. and redistribution of power increases liberty; centralisation always involves the risk, and for those who rule the temptation, of total domination. Germany's second chamber, composed of representatives of the governments of the *Länder*, the states, has been mentioned already. Were there ever to be an extreme central government in Germany, it would undoubtedly have to contend with a recalcitrant and on the whole, in the balance of its parts, moderate second chamber. In any case, even if a party fails to win two or even three successive federal elections, it is likely to form several *Land* governments, so that its frustration remains limited. Moreover, wherever there is a federal system, there have to be ways of mediating between the two powers. A federal system, as the minority of the Kilbrandon Commission on the Constitution observed during the British devolution debate, implies almost of necessity legal institutions which guard the constitution. For some, this is an argument against it; for many, it strengthens the case in favour.

But when all this is said it is still not done. Indeed, one suspects that while there will be considerable noise about devolution in future years, nothing much will actually happen. The nations of Scotland and Wales will keep their cultural differences as well as their minister in London; some counties, especially in the North, will maintain a sense of identity; but otherwise Westminster will continue to rule. This makes it all the more important that local government should be strong, and should be seen to be strong. The latter consideration is no minor one. British local government is curiously impersonal. The mayor is a ceremonial figure without power; the town clerk or his equivalent has power, but is not elected; and the leader of the majority of the council, who is elected, and has power, is usually a pale party politician. If Britain had directly elected mayors who combine the functions of the present mayor with those of the town clerk and to some extent the majority leader, then people would know who is in charge where they live. There might well be a stronger sense of responsibility, both on the part of those in power and of the community at large. In any case, local government would be removed from the bureaucratic detachment in which it exists, and would begin to make sense. People might even vote in larger numbers.

Having political mayors, directly elected, is more than a procedural gimmick; but it may be regarded as too alien to the British tradition to have any chance of implementation. In that case, the relation between local and central government becomes crucial. In Britain, this relationship is somewhere half-way between the American system of local autonomy and the French system of total local dependence. But the balance is changing. George Jones and John Stewart, who were both members of the Layfield Committee on Local Government Finance, make the point that through the 1980 Local Government, Planning and Land Act, and central government practice with respect to rate support grants, the constitution has been changed in favour of Westminster.[2] The Secretary of State can intervene in local decisions even at the stage of estimates. 'The Government seems poised to take a gigantic leap towards direct central control over local authorities, destroying the basis of local self-government.' Some may like this; after all, it confirms the sovereignty of Westminster. But Jones and Stewart make the opposite case. They argue for 'a vital and viable local government system, which can set up countervailing pressures to the centre, not to overwhelm it, but to provide balancing forces'. The main instrument for the creation of such a system is 'local accountability, by which [the Layfield Committee] meant the clear responsibility of local authority for its own financial decisions'. Jones and Stewart would like to see this division of powers almost entrenched in law, if not in a constitution. They also argue that proportional representation would increase accountability. Whatever the way forward, the basic argument has a great deal to be said for it: a modern society fares best if it offers as much decentralisation as possible, and retains only as much power for central government as is necessary. If this is true, then the unitary state of Britain leaves much to be desired.

This raises a question which we have raised before: whatever happened to the barons? Is there not a history of decentralised authority to which the country could, and perhaps should, return? The answer is not simple. Baronial power was hardly the power of local authorities. As the barons joined forces to establish central authorities, they applied their own, non-democratic experience to the country as a whole. In fact, the central state has not grown out of local or regional units in Britain. Britain has always been a highly centralised society.

This experience is mitigated only by the fact that the barons did not yield all their powers to the central state, nor did they themselves have total power in their bailiwicks. While Britain is, and has been, a centralised society, much of what mattered to people was, and is, not done by government at all. In other words, not only central government, but government in general is still less important in Britain than in other European countries. There is still much that is not regulated. There are wide areas in which people help themselves. Britain is one of the few countries where an inactive government would not lead to a state of shock – indeed most shocks emanate from government activity – but would rather enable people to get on with things. In this sense, too, the whole superstructure of Westminster and Whitehall is but a game. Real things are done by a real people in real circumstances rather than by the great powerhouse of abstraction.

Chapter Fifteen
THE POLITICS OF ECONOMIC DECLINE

There is no lack of evidence to show that the Westminster game is carried on in mid-air, with those whom the players are supposed to represent playing at best the role of somewhat bored onlookers. Many in fact have turned away, and confine themselves to expressing their disinterest, if not disgust, whenever the opportunity presents itself. The most obvious opportunity is of course a general election. For some time after the war, general elections showed growing support for the two-party system and thus, one assumes, for their adversary game. But in the 1950s, such support began to wane. Whereas in 1951, the two major parties of the time received nearly ninety-seven per cent of the votes cast, their share was reduced to a mere seventy-five per cent in October 1974. In 1979, it rose slightly to eighty-one per cent; though in that election Labour had its lowest poll since 1931, and the Conservatives won a majority of seventy-one seats with forty-four per cent of the vote, which was less than they had had in 1970.

Voting for other parties is of course open to interpretation. Still, a number of statements about the Liberal vote are probably safe. It is first of all a vote against the two-party system, as well as against its two protagonists. It is therefore a vote for constitutional change. It is also a vote, if the notion makes sense, for active moderation, that is to say, for moderate policies which are nevertheless represented with some gusto. Very largely, the Liberal vote is undoubtedly a protest vote. If and when proportional representation is introduced, it may well decline somewhat. Similarly, there was probably an element of protest in the vote for the Nationalist parties in Scotland and Wales. They too were unlikely to form a government, so that they permitted an expression of dissent as well as one of identification. Either way, in the last decade, a quarter of the electorate has actively expressed its discontent with the Westminster game. Another quarter, of course, did not vote at all.

This is not to say that the remaining half are particularly happy with what their representatives do. Richard Rose found from opinion research 'that the policy preferences of MPs . . . differ from those who elect them..[1] For one thing, not surprisingly, MPs show a greater degree of cohesion in policy matters than voters do. Every voter has, as it were, his or her own mix of preferences and beliefs. But sometimes, the lack of congruence between voters and representatives reaches striking dimensions. On the issue of 'higher income tax rather then higher purchase tax', raised by a Conservative government in 1971, only twenty-eight per cent of the Conservative voters agreed with their government, whereas sixty per cent disagreed on the other hand, forty-two per cent of all Labour voters agreed, and forty-one per cent disagreed. The example may be extreme, but the principle which it raises it not. In Britain as in other countries, the electorate concentrates in quite large majorities around what might be called middle-of-the-road policies. It dislikes seeing issues turnèd into political footballs. A random audience is most likely to applaud views which straddle party lines, especially if they are accompanied by a mild attack on those party lines. Thus, a centrist electorate is faced with the spectacle of an adversary system. It is not likely to be shocked by the corporate underpinnings of the adversary game.

Such straightforward data would lead one to assume a degree of disenchantment among the British electorate. The assumption is confirmed by a much more specific and thorough study of the relationship between political attitudes and economic development in Britain. James E. Alt, in his book *The Politics of Economic Decline*, in which he analyses opinion research data for Britain since 1964, distinguishes between people's 'individual economic outlook' and their 'national economic outlook'. In other words, he finds that people have not only a view of how they themselves are doing, but also one of how the country is doing. As he applies this distinction to Britain in the 1960s James Alt makes a strange discovery. On the one hand, people find that they themselves are doing rather well; on the other hand, they believe that the country is doing badly. 'National economic outlook is largely independent of personal outlook.'[2] More surprising still, if one thinks of the assumptions which governments make about voting behaviour, people's political views are not determined by their personal economic outlook. It is as if people's actual economic position was almost irrelevant to their political behaviour. Voting and party preferences are determined by how they see the country going. If one speculates further that people's views of how the country is going may well be influenced by their party preferences, an almost circular consequence emerges: people vote for a party because they believe that it will improve the economic outlook of the country, the features of which this party has itself determined.

But this discovery is tied to a period in which things were still going relatively well. At any rate, there were no dramatic indicators of deterioration in the 1960s. In the 1970s, this condition changed. First, there was inflation, later to be followed by unemployment, by years of declining real wages, and by visible signs of decline. Not surprisingly, the national and the personal economic outlook began to converge in this period. Moreover, people began to expect government to do something about the economy. But they were disappointed, and surely there is some relationship between this disappointment and the wider political disenchantment expressed in general elections. 'In 1970, nearly sixty per cent felt that "a government can do a lot to check rising prices". In early 1974, only a quarter of the electorate felt that way, while the great majority felt that "prices would go on rising fast no matter what any government tries to do".'[3] The converse of this is, of course, that people no longer blame government for inflation; they have become 'realists', as Alt likes to put it.

Alt's study was completed in 1978; most of his material dates back to 1974 and earlier. Perhaps this has to be taken into account so far as unemployment is concerned. In this respect, Alt finds, people still expect government to do something. Moreover, this expectation is not based on self-interest. 'Preferring reduced unemployment is an altruistic policy choice, since reducing unemployment will by and large serve to alleviate the suffering of others.'[4] Today, if one adds to the already unemployed those who are fearful of unemployment, self-interest is more likely to be dominant.

In any case, the general issue of disenchantment is not affected by this difference. James Alt notes that in 1974, 'the average Labour and Conservative voters are not located all that far apart', and that in any case a majority of all voters are not very strongly attached to the party which receives their vote.[5] Between 1966 and 1974, there has been, as Alt puts it, a 'dramatic decline in instrumental voting'. People no longer expect their parties to deliver; they vote for them out of a more or less vague feeling of attachment. One suspects that after the 1978/79 winter of discontent, 'instrumental voting' rose again for a short period, though it is quite likely that this period was very short indeed. Still, there is one finding of Alt's study which sounds almost like a prediction of the 1979 election. He speaks of the 'odd situation' that 'in personal "hard times" strong Conservatives become even stronger Conservatives, while on the Labour side those with the strongest identification run into the dilemma of lessened support for social welfare policies and thus for the party itself'.[6]

More generally, however, the 'trend towards partisan decline and de-alignment' has probably continued.[7] James Alt himself takes the story to 1976, and concludes: 'In large measure, then, the story of the mid 1970s is the story of a politics of declining expectations. People attached a great deal of importance to economic problems, people saw clearly the developments that were taking place, and people expected developments in advance and thus were able to discount the impact of the worst of them. However, in unprecedented numbers, people also ceased to expect the election of their party to make them better off, largely because they also ceased to expect it to be able to do very much about what they identified as the principal economic problems of the time. The result of this . . . was not a politics of protest, but a politics of quiet disillusion, a politics in which lack of involvement or indifference to organised party politics was the most important feature.'[8]

There are two conclusions which one can draw from these findings, and though they are not altogether compatible, both seem to have come true. One is that there will be an increasing dissociation of electoral views from the Westminster game. People will try to fend for themselves. The opportunities of the black economy are much more important for them than any specific measure promised by a political party. The party game becomes more and more irrelevant. Intensity of party support tends towards zero. The overwhelming desire is to be left alone by government. There are certainly signs that this is happening already.

The other conclusion is that disenchantment is in the first instance caused by the Westminster game as it is played at the moment. Since government is inevitable, and since most people would like to see a government with which they can identify to some extent, even if it does not satisfy their 'instrumental' expectations, people look for change. There is widespread awareness today that a change in the electoral system would have wider ramifications. But above all, the spectrum of political options has become wider. Some of the new options are extreme; they fit better into the adversary than into a consensus model. Judging from available evidence, their only hope of victory is through one of the recognised parties, that is, as a wolf in sheep's clothing. But another new option is not extreme. Indeed its only clear policy for the time being is its moderation. Evidently, Social Democrats, and even more so, Social Democrats and Liberals in alliance, have found a gap in the political market. They respond to the doubts as well as the hopes of a large number of voters. The question is whether the change which they promise is real, and above all, whether it manages to deal with the real issues of the country, or is just another expectation raised to be disappointed.

Chapter Sixteen
SOME STEPS FORWARD

In looking back over this section, it strikes me that it has turned into a litany of criticism. This was not intended, though it reflects the current debate in Britain. For if there is any reason to have doubts about Britain's institutions, it is the extent to which they have come under pressure. Party manifestos, books and pamphlets, Reith and Dimbleby Lectures, newspaper articles, political speeches, all advocate fundamental changes in Britain's constitution. This is not a good sign. A constitution is at its best when it is not debated at all. If proposals for reform sprout all over, there is usually something wrong. Yet it is important to see such faults in proportion.

For one thing, we have stressed the ability of Britain's political institutions to accommodate change, quite apart from the liveliness and topicality of debate which makes even an unrepresentative parliament a mirror of the nation. These strengths are not to be underestimated. However, there is another of even greater importance. Some years ago, the Trilateral Commission, a self-appointed group of distinguished individuals from Europe, the United States and Japan (hence 'trilateral'), debated what in the published volume came to be called *The Crisis of Democracy*.[1] Many members were agreed that democracy was under pressure. The reasons they gave were varied; but perhaps the most important of all was that suggested by Sam Huntington.

Huntington argued, here as elsewhere, that democracy has to be a positive-sum game if it is to work. In his view, it is based on politicians fulfilling at least some of their promises. If they can no longer do so, that is, at times of economic decline, then democracy itself is at risk. The commission shared Huntington's forebodings, and perhaps his implicit recommendation of more authoritarian forms of government as well.

Yet Britain had shown already that it was possible to keep democratic institutions alive at times of economic decline. Indeed, the real politics of economic decline in Britain is the achievement of democracy as a negative-sum game. There are not many countries – to that extent Huntington and the Trilateral Commission are probably right – which can hope to deal with adverse economic circumstances in a similarly liberal way. Liberty and openness are deeply entrenched in Britain.

It is in the light of this observation that reforms of Britain's political system should be seen. Such reforms must not be aimed to overturn tradition altogether. They must, on the contrary, build on tradition and concentrate on relatively minor, but strategic changes.

One such minor, but strategic, change is electoral reform. To those who have taken part in the heated debate in recent years, it may sound surprising to hear it called minor. Yet all they have to do is cast an eye on the history of electoral systems in Britain.[2] Until 1885, constituencies had as a rule two or three members, and a variety of voting systems were tried. In 1885, a law was enacted to create single-member seats in most places; but there was much opposition. George Goschen raised a point which we have not discussed here, though it has in fact become a regrettable characteristic of Britain's political geography: 'Let us beware that the single-member constituencies do not develop into one-class constituencies, whose members will come here feeling themselves responsible, not to the people of the whole country, but to the particular class living in the district by which they are returned.' The Proportional Representation Society remained strong and saw to it that the debate over the electoral system did not die down. At last, in 1905, the debate became official. A Royal Commission was set up. Promises of change were made by leaders. A Speaker's Conference was convened. By 1918, after more than a decade of debate, it looked as if change was imminent. However, after a series of confusing votes without impressive majorities for any position, the 1918 election overtook reformers. The 1885 system remained in force. But as one considers the inter-war years, and the war years until 1945, one must not forget that they fall into two halves, one in which (as has been shown) three parties competed with each other, and another in which a coalition governed the country. It was after 1945 that the practice, and the ideology of the first-past-the-post system grew to full fruition; and this fruition was short-lived, for by 1951, support for the system began to decline.

Michael Steed makes an important statement about electoral

systems: 'The truth is that the effects of any electoral system reflect a delicate balance of its undoubted mechanical effects, its more questionable psychological effects, the nature of party conflict and the history of the evolution of both party and voting systems.'[3] The importance of this statement is its implication that no one system is appropriate at all times. There may have been times when the British plurality system was entirely appropriate. But if we examine Steed's criteria today, the picture looks less impressive. The mechanical effects of the system not only tend to translate tiny changes into major shifts, but also remove the parties from prevailing views. The psychological effects, that is to say, people's propensity not to 'waste' votes, have probably never worked. The nature of party conflict changed at the very moment at which there was a relatively small, but nation-wide Liberal party, let alone more recently, when the Social Democratic Party was founded. Steed himself adds to his statement: 'In 1974 in Britain that balance broke down.' Certainly, recent years have seen a new ball game to which the old rules were no longer adequate.

There are other arguments for the plurality system, by which the first past the post wins all, which no longer hold. It is said that the system produces clear majorities; but in fact there have been minority governments, and it would not be surprising if 1974, or 1978–79 happened again in future parliaments. It is said that the system makes coalitions worked out in smoke-filled rooms unnecessary; but by 1981 it is clear that both major parties are themselves highly complicated coalitions which debate their differences partly in public but largely behind the closed doors of rooms which may or may not be smoke-filled. In any case, the British aversion to coalition is strange. Nevil Johnson is probably right that the 'overall effect' of coalition would be 'less heat and more light'. And why not? Why not 'compel those who engage in political argument and discussion . . . to recognise more fully the complexity and difficulty of many of the issues they deal with'?[4] Is not, in terms of quality of argument and level of debate, the House of Lords a better model than the House of Commons? And are there not frequent, though admittedly ad hoc, coalitions in the House of Lords? It is said that the British plurality system produces stability; but in fact only three parliaments since the war have lived out their full term, and on at least three other occasions new elections had to be called within a year, which is not the case in countries with proportional representation and fixed-term parliaments.

There remains one significant point. Whatever the weaknesses of Parliament may be in relation to governing the country, it has an important role to play in establishing, or casting doubt on, the legitimacy of government, and of political institutions in general. The link between a Member of Parliament and his or her constituents is important, however tenuous it may be, both in large rural, and concentrated but ill-defined urban, constituencies. It would clearly not be desirable to shift from the plurality system to one of national party lists and total proportionality as it exists, say, in Israel. But there are alternatives. In 1976, the Hansard Society Commission on Electoral Reform suggested a British variant of the German mixed system; this variant would mean that in future, as in the past, all members of parliament are elected in constituencies.[5] One-half, or even two-thirds of the members would gain their seats as at present, that is by a plurality of votes in a constituency. But an overall allocation of seats would then be made on the basis of national percentage polls, perhaps ruling out parties which poll less than five per cent or fewer than three first-round seats overall; and members would be chosen from the 'best losers' in constituencies. Thus, if the Liberal Party were to be entitled to 60 seats, but had gained only 10, up to 50 Liberals who have done best in their constituencies. If the notion of the 'best losers' getting into Parliament is too alien to the British tradition, there are other alternatives. Multi-member constituencies are, as we have seen, not alien to the British tradition. There are various ways in which two, three, even five members can be elected in most constituencies: by 'single transferable vote'; by regional list; by counting preferences.

Whichever system is chosen, electoral reform along these lines would change the character of the Westminster game. It would take some of the irrelevant adversary features out of politics. It would help re-establish legitimacy. But it would not transform out of recognition British politics, let alone its objective, the welfare of the people. More continuity would probably increase confidence and thereby have a helpful effect on economic development. But neither the long-term problems of Britain's economy nor the conflicts between employers and labour would go away just because there would be coalitions and more stable governments. The issue of wages, productivity, profits and investments, and of course that of prices which is related to the others, remains. A way has to be found to deal with it.

Since the suggestion advanced here with respect to squaring the employer-labour circle is likely to be even more controversial than that of electoral reform, it may be useful to have a glance at other countries. In Germany there was until recently, and apart from all other consensus mechanisms, an arrangement called 'concerted action'. It consisted of regular meetings convened by government, in which the equivalent of the TUC and the CBI participated. These meetings were not intended to reach decisions, though 'guidelines' for wages and other developments were discussed. Their purpose was essentially to reach a common assessment of the state of the economy. From this, most guidelines for behaviour followed naturally. More recently, the 'concerted action' in the Department of Economic Affairs has been replaced by talks with the Federal Chancellor which have the same effect. In Switzerland, there is a long-term agreement, now more than fifty years old, which stipulates an 'obligation for industrial peace'. This works because again there are mechanisms for bringing about an agreed assessment of economic conditions, and guidelines which are seen to be beneficial, and fair, by all. The 'Swedish model' worked for as long as the group of economic experts of unions and employers (the so-called 'EFO group') was able to agree on a norm for wages policy. It was when, in the mid 1970s, the EFO system broke down that the Swedish model itself began to be threatened.[6]

Such stories could be multiplied. Almost every European country provides an illustration, peculiar to its own social tradition, of the attempt to introduce an element of predictability into the inevitable conflicts of management and labour, as well as government and industry. What these stories show is that economic relationships have enhanced the welfare of countries wherever there was a mechanism for doing three things: first, to bring about a common assessment of economic conditions and prospects; secondly, to introduce the interests represented by elected governments into the disputes of industry; and thirdly, to grope for possible guidelines of action for all concerned.

There is, to be sure, one contrary example. It is provided by the United States of America. In America there may be local, or even industry-wide agreements, as in the case of the communications industry; but by and large the core relationships of the economy are governed by what some would call market forces. Real wages not only rise, but they fall, and they have fallen for several successive years in the last decade. Unemployment remains an effective threat for all. Air controllers can be sacked by the President when they go on strike, because they are public employees. In other words, the ancient human emotions of fear and greed regulate the level of wages and profits as well as productivity and investment. It must be added that this took place, and perhaps still takes place, in the framework of economic positive-sum games, that is, under circumstances under which there continued to be more for all. Indeed, the desire to keep playing this game, to work towards creating an ever bigger cake for redistribution, is the underlying motive for letting market forces have free play.

But Britain is a European country. However much some may be tempted to conjure up the American example, the truth is that real wages are in fact if not in law pegged against a downward trend, that employment protection is highly developed, that governments would find it difficult to sack public employees merely because they go on strike, and of course that people do not think of their conflicts as being a part of a vast economic positive-sum game in which everyone wins. As a result, conflicts in Europe are not only tougher, but less individualised. They are not resolved by personal success, but by collective advances. Value judgments apart, these are facts which any attempt to square the circle of economic interests on the part of different groups has to take into account. Since it does not look as if the basic cultural facts, that is people's prevailing attitudes, will change, economic stability has to be achieved with the grain rather than against it. This in turn means that ways must be found to bring the constituent forces of economic conflicts together. Some kind of social contract is imperative.

Words like these have become loaded with memories, and with prejudice. Let it be clear, therefore, that the social contract between Harold Wilson and Jack Jones is not what I have in mind. At the time, this was a contract by which the unions accepted wage restraint, and in exchange they were given influence on legislation, and on government policy generally. To some extent, this contract marked the abdication of elective government. Clearly, a modern government will not wantonly ignore the interests of large organisations, be they unions, employers, farmers, war veterans, disabled people, civil rights organisations. Equally clearly, the role of parliamentary government is more than that of an honest broker between organised interests. Government represents the interests of citizens as citizens, that is in respects which transcend all particular interests. The social contract *á la* Wilson marks the climax and incipient decline of the corporate bias old-style, that is, of government by interest groups. The contract which is advocated here is fundamentally different. It is not intended to turn the state into a corporate web, but to introduce the element of generalised interest represented by government into economic affairs. Thus the bias is not corporate but consensual, and it concerns not the state but the economy.

What exactly does this mean? One may think of NEDO, the National Economic Development Office, in this connection. It is not the worst mechanism for achieving the necessary economic contract. One may also think of less formalised arrangements, such as regular meetings convened by the Prime Minister. In any case, the three tasks mentioned earlier as having been recognised by all successful European economies have to be achieved. There have to be regular meetings in order to define the main issues of the economic condition. This is not easy. It requires expertise as well as persuasion. Even so, it remains threatened by the obvious conflicts of interests: employers will insist that wages are too high; unions will criticize profits and demand investment, public and private; government will invoke international problems. However, some raprochement in the definition of issues is a condition of progress. There will then have to be an input of government interest. By that is meant not only the interest of government as an employer, and thus its own indication of where it can go, but above all a reminder of the overall concern of the country. The future of social services, for example, is an issue which has to be introduced into joint discussions by government. Finally, there is a need to reach at least procedural conclusions on guidelines for action. This is clearly the most precarious item in the execution of any social contract. It is incidentally not necessarily the most important. If there is a common understanding of issues, even a common definition of major problems, a framework of action is created which by itself forms a guideline. However, from time to time, it may well be necessary to try and reach agreement about rates of increases in wages, or joint efforts at increasing investment, or taxation.

A social, or better, perhaps, an economic, contract of this kind may seem underdefined and precarious. Indeed it is. It is not a statutory incomes policy which presupposes that Parliament can actually regulate industrial conflict. It is not an indirect incomes policy by taxation which also overlooks the fact that conflicts are not the invention of malevolent leaders, but are built into the system – any system – of economic organisation. Insofar as the arrangement proposed here relies on institutions, they are most likely to be forms of arbitration as proposed by

James Meade in his book on *Wage-Fixing*. But essentially we are talking about an orientation, a direction of action by all concerned. The main constraint built into this orientation is an obligation on government to convene the economic actors regularly and with the kind of agenda which follows from this argument.

Has it not all been tried before? Has it not failed in the past, so that it is bound to fail again? It is a rather amusing, if costly, characteristic of British politics that anything that has been tried before, and has not worked to perfection, is ruled out for the future. In fact, life is complicated. The attempt to bring together protagonists of the great battles of our world is bound to fail every now and again. Its failure cannot sensibly be interpreted as a justification for not trying again. On the contrary, the more the attempt at introducing sense and predictability into economic development fails, the harder one has to try and try again. The economic contract is an essential of progress, indeed even of stability, in this field.

There is a footnote to this suggestion which links it with a third step forward. The footnote concerns trade unions. Any social contract cements union power, if it does not enhance it. The question is therefore whether there are any limits to this power. Legislation has not been particularly effective, though in certain areas it is probably necessary. But there is another way. Keith Middlemas has indicated its course in a comment on the government Green Paper by the Employment Secretary, James Prior. Middlemas assumes plausibly that it is 'inherently improbable that only one side is to blame for the present mess'.[7] This is an argument against legislation directed at one side only. On the other hand, there is the old British principle of self-regulation. 'Self-regulation is the only complete answer.' It has been tried in other institutions, notably in the City; it also takes up an 'old strand in TUC history'. Indeed, 'self-regulation sums up what most trade union leaders define as their own approach to the political system'. Once the principle is accepted, there could be 'a new and fruitful political discourse' between government and the unions. Unions could be asked to reply to questions about their internal structure, secret ballots, and the like; having to answer such questions might be an inducement to act. But there should be no attempt to tilt the balance of industrial power by legislation. 'Consent has been out of fashionable political discourse for too long. Self-regulation offers a way to slow down the pendulum before the law is made a pawn in the struggle over powers quite different from immunity in strikes.'

This cannot mean, of course, that the law has no function at all. So far, steps forward have been discussed which are not really changes of direction. They build on traditional values and institutions of Britain, and develop them to cope with new sets of problems. As we come to a final strategic step forward, this is no longer so clearly the case. There is an argument for enhancing the rule of the law in Britain. In discussing class, and again party, we have tried to show that there has been a change from collective and solidary action to individual action. Individual interests are complex, and situational; but they are real. Parties no longer represent individuals in their entirety, or even all their interests. In an important sense, the individual has become the main actor on the political scene. But how can the individual act in a world of giants? The individual looks a little like the quaint little Trinity Church at the end of the overpowering skyscrapers of Wall Street. Trinity Church has priests, and presumably environmentalists to protect it. But who protects the individual? This is where the law, and more particularly the issue of a Bill of Rights, have their role.

The issue has been introduced into public debate by one of the great judges of the time, Lord Scarman, in his Hamlyn Lectures of 1974 on *English Law – The New Dimension*. There, Lord Scarman went so far as to make 'tentative', but precise and significant, 'proposals'. '(1) A new constitutional settlement replacing that of 1689 to be worked out by Parliament, the judges, the Law Commissions, and the Government through a phased programme of study, research, and extensive consultation; (2) The basis of the new settlement should be entrenched provisions (including a Bill of Rights), and restraint upon administrative and legislative power, protecting it from attack by a bare majority in Parliament. . .'[8] Elsewhere in the lectures, Scarman makes the case for incorporating a declaration of fundamental rights into English law, and protecting these rights from all encroachments, including those of the State, and of Parliament. In a subsequent discussion, Lord Scarman became somewhat more specific and suggested that the Bill of Rights should include 'first of all due process, natural justice, rules of procedure', but secondly, 'some substantive rights', and also, 'guiding principles to assist the judges'.[9]

Why should there be a Bill of Rights? What are its advantages? Leslie Scarman concentrates very largely on two arguments. One is what he calls the 'international challenge', that is, the existence of the United Nations Charter and the European Convention of Human Rights. The other argument has to do with what Lord Hailsham, in his Dimbleby Lecture of 1976, called the 'elective dictatorship' of Britain, that is, the sovereignty of Parliament and the fact that courts can under no circumstances overrule, let alone annul, statutes. 'It is the helplessness of law in face of the legislative sovereignty of Parliament which makes it difficult for the legal system to accommodate the concept of fundamental and inviolable human rights.'[10] In a subsequent discussion, organised by Timothy Raison at the Centre for Studies in Social Policy in 1975, Lord Scarman added an even more fundamental point: 'My own philosophical position is that I believe there are certain human rights and duties which not even the politicians by a majority in one house of Parliament have the right to undermine.'[11] In that discussion I expressed the view that the demand for a Bill of Rights showed itself a breakdown of consensus, and that it was to be hoped that this consensus would be reconstituted. In the meantime, I have become more doubtful about such a reconstitution, and therefore more inclined to favour a Bill of Rights. Timothy Raison's point remains valid, however, when he says: 'A new Bill of Rights – or any major constitutional change – could in my view only work if it were based on consensus.'[12] It must not be regarded as a weapon in the hands of one side to prevent the other from doing things for which it has a majority.

A Bill of Rights, that is a set of guarantees of fundamental individual rights which is entrenched and incorporated in law, is probably the only way in which the individual can defend himself or herself against the overpowering institutions of modern society. Government and Parliament are by no means the only such institutions, although it is important that it should be possible for the individual to call on the courts to defend himself or herself against administrative decisions, and against statutes for that matter. But there are certain other issues which can also best, and perhaps only, be dealt with by having recourse to individual rights. Take the closed shop. Legislation geared to trade unions and their action is awkward not merely because it is difficult to enforce, but because it misses the point. The issue of the closed shop is not primarily one of desirable or undesirable union policies, but one of the rights of the individual to resist the force of organisations and, for example, to work without becoming a member of anything. To have made this point is the great merit of the European Court on Human Rights when it invoked Article 11 of the European Convention in order to confirm the right of three British Rail employees not to join a union.

The Court stated explicitly that 'it is not called upon to review the closed shop system as such'; but it then insisted that the individual 'right to freedom of peaceful assembly and to freedom of association' implies the right not to join an association. 'The situation facing the applicants clearly runs counter to the concept of freedom of association in the negative sense.' Compulsion to join a union in order to get or keep employment is therefore a violation of Article 11 of the European Convention.[13]

The European Convention is not a part of British law, so that the rulings of the Court are not legally binding. But they constitute an important part of what Lord Scarman calls the 'international challenge' to British law. Once again, this challenge is not one of restricting the operation of particular organisations or instances as such; it is one of guaranteeing individual rights. Thus, the Bill of Rights would be equally applicable if it was not a union insisting on membership, but, say, an employer who insists that his employees should be members of a 'moral majority' American-style. It is in order to defend certain rights which neither politicians nor anyone else have a right to undermine that a Bill of Rights makes sense. It may indeed be the most important single change of Britain's institutions.

For make no mistake, this is a significant change. Lord Scarman is well aware of the fact that his proposals mark a major departure from tradition. This is why he not only refers to the Magna Carta and the Bill of Rights of 1689, but also to Britain's international commitments. A Bill of Rights requires, if not a supreme court, then a court which deals with new kinds of legal matter. It makes the diminution of the rights of Parliament explicit. It bids farewell to the British principle of keeping the law out of disputes between social and political groups. Indeed, it ascribes to the law and thereby to lawyers, functions to which they are quite unaccustomed. Perhaps Michael Zander is right that such a major departure should first be tried not by way of entrenchment, but as a simple act of Parliament.[14] In this way, the risk of divisiveness which rightly worries Timothy Raison could be reduced. But this is a tactical question. The fact remains that, to quote Leslie Scarman yet again, the common law is at the end of its tether. Parliament is the wrong instrument to deal with certain individual rights, and the philosophical anchoring of these rights can no longer be taken for granted in Britain. Change is happening, change is necessary; it may as well be channelled in ways which serve the individual and his or her life chances.

EUROPE, AND OTHER LINKS WITH THE WORLD

Chapter Seventeen
A QUESTION OF IDENTITY

The dream of parliamentary sovereignty is as touching as it is irrelevant. One may regret its irrelevance, but unless one closes one's eyes to the world one cannot deny it. Domestically, Parliament shares its powers with the other members of the corporate triangle, and with many outside them. Internationally, Parliament shares its powers with the rest of the world. This is true whether Britain opts in or opts out, is a member of international organisations or prefers splendid isolation. Sovereignty today is very largely shared sovereignty, and countries have a role in this process to the extent to which they understand its principle.

To many in Britain, this is not exactly news. Whether they put it in these terms or not, they know that not only cars and insurance policies, but inflation and unemployment, too, can be imported, and, of course, exported. But some of the most vocal spokesmen in British politics are not prepared to accept the realities of the world today. They are to be found on the far right as well as the far left. When the House of Commons voted on the question of joining the European Community in 1971, Enoch Powell implored the House not to say aye, because to do so would be an 'irrevocable decision to part with the sovereignty of this House and to commit ourselves to the merger of this nation and its destinies with the rest of the Community'; it would be a 'vote against the vital principle by which this House exists'.[1] Tony Benn gives this theory his own twist: 'The parliamentary democracy we have developed and established in Britain is based, not upon the sovereignty of Parliament, but upon the sovereignty of the people who, by exercising their vote, lend their sovereign powers to members of Parliament, to use on their behalf for the duration of a single Parliament only.' But this is said in the same context, of Britain's membership of the European Community, and in the light of the conclusion that the delegated 'powers . . . must be returned intact to the electorate to whom they belong': 'Continued membership of the Community would, therefore, mean the end of Britain as a completely self-governing nation and of our democratically elected Parliament as the supreme law-making body of the United Kingdom.'[2]

Such statements would be unthinkable in most other countries, and perhaps in all. William Wallace is right to observe, in his *Illusion of Sovereignty*, that 'the British and the French are preoccupied with the idea of sovereignty to an extent unparalleled elsewhere in Western Europe'; he is even right to note that 'impassioned defenders are to be found at the two ends of the conventional political spectrum: Gaullists and Communists in France, ultra-Tories and Tribune Group MPs in Britain'.[3] But there is an important difference. In France, sovereignty means the sovereignty of the nation, never mind whether it is Napoleon or Louis Philippe, de Gaulle or Mendes-France who speaks for it. In Britain, sovereignty means the sovereignty of Parliament which is of course the parliament of the unitary state of Britain. Thus, democracy comes before the nation, or rather, the nation is defined by its democratically elected Parliament.

This is an admirable notion. Nevertheless, it fails to describe the realities of the world in which we are living. Take money as an example. As Lord Kaldor rightly pointed out before Harold Wilson's devaluation of 1967, determining the value of one's currency is one of the prime expressions of 'complete self-government'. It must not be that American interest rates, or a flight from the French franc, or the German inflation rate, or a rush of speculative currency movements, affect the value of the pound sterling. But are we really to believe that what must not be, cannot be? The plain fact is that reality does not tally with the notion of complete self-government. The pound is infinitely dependent on what happens in other economies, and what is done by other governments. Moreover, this dependence is mutual. If a government with a protectionist programme were to be elected in Britain, this would affect not only the pound, but indirectly, and in different directions, other currencies as well. And if Britain were to decide, say, to leave the International Monetary Fund, it would merely forgo the chance to influence the course of events, but would still be influenced by them.

Money is but one example of shared sovereignty as it dominates the modern world. Defence, trade, energy, investment are others. But there are some, many perhaps, in Britain who do not want to take the point. There are at least three reasons why this should be so. One is the tradition of parliamentary sovereignty of which we have spoken. Another reason is the simple geographical fact that Britain is an island. It is hard to exaggerate the importance of this. One does not need to travel from the Hook of Holland to Harwich in the bowels of a troop transporter to become aware of it. The consequence of Britain's insular quality are literally ubiquitous. Rabies, or its absence, is both an important fact of life – at least of the lives of animals – and a symbol; no Continental country could hope to keep it off its territory. Driving on the left would hardly be possible in a country which admits thousands of cars every day by road; even Sweden, where access by road is not easy, has found it necessary to switch to driving on the right. Greenwich Mean Time may have become a standard for others, but it lags an hour behind Central European Time. There are profound differences in Customs procedures and customs in general. The notion of a Channel tunnel, or a bridge, is both obvious at a time at which it is technologically and financially feasible, and abhorrent to many in Britain. Such abhorrence may well have deep roots. It is not simply because of an imaginary fear that one night a Continental invasion force may take Fortress Britain by surprise; the British are not silly. But there is a widespread gut feeling that a tunnel, or a bridge, whould mean that Britain ceases to be an island; and this, people certainly do not want.

Some islands connect, some separate. Britain does both. Like the Greek island states of antiquity – much smaller to be sure, but existing at a time at which distances were much harder to overcome – Britain has both maintained its independence and engaged in lively exchanges of trade with others. At times, and even at difficult times, such trade originated in far-away places. During the wars, convoys had to bring food to an island which has reduced its agricultural production to a level far below self-sufficiency. In other words, the island has deliberately made itself dependent on others, as well as making others dependent on it. However, as one looks more closely, one finds that such dependence remained largely confined to a well-defined circle of suppliers and buyers. The Empire, and its first revolutionary renegade, the United States of America, by and large defined the boundaries of Britain's intensive commercial relations with the world.

Politically, this was not so. In the later nineteenth century, splendid isolation, that is, abstinence from matters arising outside the English-speaking world, became increasingly difficult. Gladstone and Disraeli fought many a memorable battle of words over Britain's involvement in Continental and Middle Eastern affairs. Whatever Disraeli's doubts, the involvement took place. The Crimean War was the beginning of a series of wars in which Britain's participation documents an extended rather than an immediate self-interest. These wars also drew Britain closer to Europe; they reminded it of its essentially European destiny.

Living on an island has obvious advantages. One of them is that people need not worry about the boundaries of their country. (Or are there still lingering doubts north of the border?) Countries are rather abstract entities; and yet they have something to do with people's sense of identity. People feel they belong; and the more sure they are of where their country begins and ends, the more confident is their sense of belonging. Germany has always been a vague concept. For one thing, it has never been identical with the political boundaries of the country. These boundaries were always narrower than the 'German nation'. As a result, there has been, for many decades if not centuries, an aggressive uncertainty about the Germans' sense of identity. It was, in fact, not a sense of identity, but a sense of self-doubt; and out of such self-doubt grew the need to try and find a fatherland which provides the security of confidence by its bigness, if not its meaning. The German case proves by contrast, as it were, the importance of the place of one's country in the world. Britain has been spared the miseries of self-doubt. Even the Irish question has not, throughout the century in which it has figured so high on the agenda of British politics, affected people's sense of identity. Indeed, the British are so sure of themselves that they can even allow a little blurring at the edges. The quaintness of the Channel Islands lies in their being a little French; the nearest railway station to Lerwick on the Shetlands is somewhere in Norway, in Bergen perhaps; and the Irish in Liverpool can vote in the national elections of both Britain and Eire.

But with all its advantages, an island is also a temptation to isolation. Insularity is the word. Such insularity becomes all the more extreme when things go badly. Economic decline is the third reason why the notion of shared sovereignty meets with so much resistance in Britain. Decline leads to fear, and fear leads to protectionism, that is, to the attempt to close oneself off from the rest of the world and try to go it alone. The prospect is not very bright. One has seen the suspect unity of employers and unions in the textile industry who ask for products from Eastern Europe and the developing countries to be kept out, so that they can continue business as usual. Their motives are fear of the future, and with it the inability to take their future into their own hands and brave the winds of change. This means adjustment by modernisation, or if need be by closing down textile mills and opening up other businesses whose prospects are better. Quite often, however, this is not happening. And there are times when one wonders whether the whole of Britain is not in danger of becoming one gigantic textile industry.

Trade protectionism is still latent in Britain, but it is not very far from the surface. Wynne Godley and his Cambridge Group of economists probably have a much wider audience than those who understand their theories of the relationship between wage-push inflation and imports. The traditional major parties not only have minorities which explicitly demand protection, but have toyed with the idea when in government. After all, why should the British consumer buy Toyotas rather than perfectly good Leyland cars which save foreign currency and provide employment at home? There is an answer; but it is also clear that the notion of hiding behind tariff walls in order to recover, and then opening one's doors again to the world, commands much support on the island.

It is nevertheless a naive notion. For one thing, Britain is in fact linked to many other countries by trade. More than thirty per cent of Britain's gross national product accrues from trade; millions are employed in export-oriented industries. There is no way in which one can have protection on the one hand and the same level of exports on the other. Secondly, the notion of getting one's economy going in splendid isolation hardly works even in developing countries. It is true that Britain has sometimes been called a 'newly developing country'; but of course it is not. An insulated British economy would soon begin to resemble an East European economy, complete with shortages, rationing, deteriorating quality, and the rest. Thirdly, there is an endearing arrogance in the belief that it is for Britain to decide, not only when to leave the international system, but when to return to it. Others may not be so prepared to accept Britain's time-scale. Indeed, trade flows may have changed for good when Britain generously makes its unilateral declaration of renewed dependence. Protectionism is, if not irreversible, then a decision with long-term consequences, and the consequences are painful. But above all, protectionism is impossible; it is as impossible as 'complete self-government'. There is no way for a major country, or perhaps any country, to opt out of the world. Oil price increases and fluctuations of the dollar have affected Eastern Europe along with the rest. Thus, interdependence is a fact.

This is also true beyond the realm of trade. Here, too, opting out is an illusion with ugly consequences. This is most clearly the case with respect to developing countries. For them, at least, Britain is a rich country. Its material and human resources could offer opportunities of welfare for many in the poor countries of the world. To some extent they do. There are examples of Britain giving a lead to others, as in the case of Zimbabwe. But there are as many examples of British governments following a sceptical public opinion rather than leading it, and telling the poor to look after themselves at least until the national house has been put in order. Here, as elsewhere, insularity may pay in the short term, though even that is doubtful; but it is not only morally indefensible, it is also impracticable in the medium term. The ostrich digging its head into the sand may not notice what happens around it, but it does not prevent it from happening by refusing to look.

The world in which we live is complicated, to state a commonplace which many are tired of hearing. But sense can be made of its complexity. This cannot be done by nostalgia, to be sure. We have to try and understand a new condition. What we see around us is not the abdication of national sovereignty, but the emergence of shared sovereignty. There are areas in which no country is 'completely self-governing', though countries are not wholly governed by others in these areas either. Instead, they govern themselves together. This means that each has a part in the government of others. It is not some internationalist idealism which brings about such sharing, but clear and present interest. No one country in Europe, France and Britain included, could hope to build an effective system of defence; thus there is NATO, an arrangement of shared sovereignty. No one country can hope to maintain a system of free trade and monetary stability; thus there are the General Agreement on Tariffs and Trade (GATT) and the International Monetary Fund (IMF) as well as European institutions to back them up at a time of crisis, and all these involve shared sovereignty. Not only does shared sovereignty not detract from power, it increases it. It liberates a country from being a passive object of the decisions of others, and involves it in matters which lie far beyond its national powers. At the same time, it takes nothing away from these national powers which is not subject in any case to external decisions and processes.

But of course, it is difficult to define one's identity in terms of shared sovereignty. This is particularly difficult at a time at which one is worried about one's future and therefore naturally tending to look inward. It takes an effort to overcome insularity and yet to satisfy the needs of people to know where they belong. This is the effort of living with complexity. Perhaps William Wallace is right that it is the task of those who are able to achieve this, to bring home to people the changed realities of interdependence. 'The realities of interdependence are not easily encapsulated in a few simple sentences, or symbolized in new slogans or catch-phrases. A considerable effort of leadership is therefore necessary to bring home to the public the strength of the contraints under which British governments are now forced to operate, and the unreality of established myths of British independence.'[4]

Chapter Eighteen
POST-IMPERIAL BRITAIN

The explanation for Britain's malaise which one hears most frequently abroad is that the country never got over losing the Empire. Somehow, when this is said, everyone around seems to find it plausible and nod. But how could losing the Empire account for economic decline and the weakening of political institutions? Some think it means a straightforward loss in national income. The colonies can no longer be exploited, and so the mother country has to rely on its own resources. This is a strange half-truth. The colonies would not have been profitable without colonisation. Malaya would hardly have known about its rubber had it not been for its British rulers, and the great companies in India and Africa were the original examples of trade creation. Others think that the lost Empire means that enterprising people no longer have anywhere to go; they are confined to the little island of Britain. This again is not very persuasive. Not only do enterprising people still find places to go, but in any case one would assume that if they stay at home they will help the economy of the country by their spirit of enterprise.

A more convincing argument has to do with the old institution of 'Imperial preferences', that is, with tariff advantages for the Empire and barriers around it. The advantage, if that is what it was, of Imperial preferences was not so much the immediate one of saving on tariffs and imports. It was, rather, the presence of guaranteed suppliers of raw materials and guaranteed markets for finished products which made the difference. But in economic affairs, such comfort is of dubious value. Among other things, it means that one does not worry too much about supplies or about exports. In particular, one does not adjust to changing demand. Demand abroad is created by the supply which is available at home. The cosy economic relationship of the Empire is precisely the kind of condition which makes for stagnation. Once the Empire crumbles, one is unprepared for the winds of competition. The Empire turns out to have been a dangerous protective mechanism.

However, even this is probably not the main effect of the Empire on its centre, Britain. This effect is, rather, moral and psychological. Those who set the tone in Britain were not only groomed to rule at home, but they practised this skill all over the world. An unusual number of people had unusual responsibilities in the four corners of the Empire. Nor was such power confined to the upper classes. Many others had at least a glimpse of the importance of the British flag in Africa and Asia, the Caribbean and the Pacific. Ever since, in the late nineteenth century, the Empire had become a national pastime rather than a vehicle for commercial companies, it was a manifest demonstration of the power and thus of the importance of Britain in the world.

If only for that reason, the loss of the Empire – a voluntary loss, to be sure, by a country which recognised the winds of change – was a painful process for Britain. The pain was increased by the way the country came to be reduced to its metropolitan core. For the second time in the century, Britain found itself the poorer at the end of a victorious war. After the First World War there had been much heartsearching about the causes of unemployment and economic decline; even politicians like Winston Churchill came to suspect world conspiracies because they were at a loss to find reasons at home. After the Second World War, the independence of India came to be a great symbolic act, though few in Britain appreciated the full significance of the symbolism. Three decades later, Britain was like almost any other medium-sized power in Europe. Gibraltar and Hong Kong and Belize and even the Falkland Islands did not make much difference. It was not so much the training ground of the upper classes that was missing as the real basis of a national sense of importance and power.

However, this history turned out to be an enormous distraction. For some time, Britain found it difficult to bring its consciousness into line with the facts of its life. The hangover of the Imperial past lasted for many years, long enough to prevent the country from finding a new place in the world. It has often been said that when Churchill made his famous Zurich speech about the need for European unification in 1946, he did not for one moment think of Britain as a part of the process. Europe, that was the others. And of course, the others went ahead, sometimes more, sometimes less, successfully, but with a fairly clear sense of direction. Britain was not a part of it. When the conference of Messina was convened in 1955, and the setting-up of a European Economic Community was decided, Britain remained aloof. Is it wrong to suspect that a lingering super-power self-image was one of the reasons?

Meanwhile, the realities of international politics have changed, and that not only in Europe. By 1980, the original fifty-one members of the United Nations had turned into 154, thirty-five of them former British colonies or dependencies. Very few of them managed to retain more than a semblance of the institutions which they had inherited. Almost all of them have gone through periods of dictatorship and one-party rule. Imperial preferences are little more than a distant memory for them; they buy, and sell, wherever the price is best. Sometimes one is reminded of the fact that Britain still has a residual function in many parts of the world. The King of Spain cancels his attendance at the Royal wedding because the newlyweds are beginning their honeymoon on the 'Britannia' in Gibraltar. The Canadian Prime Minister asks for the 'patriation' of the Canadian constitution in order to be able to make changes without having to ask Westminster. The Commonwealth Games are threatened because New Zealand had allowed the Springboks to play Rugby teams on its islands. More seriously, Britain can go to war over distant islands it may be prepared to give away, but will not have taken away. Nevertheless, Britain remains a medium-sized European power with a great history behind it.

There are other symptoms of the process. When there were widespread misgivings about IMF inspectors looking at the books of the Treasury in 1975 in order to find out whether Britain was credit-worthy, one was reminded of the origins of the institution. At the time, that is in 1944–45, British and American ideas contracted a happy, if somewhat stormy marriage. One of the ideas at the cradle of the IMF was that the pound sterling should be its reserve currency. (The notion of sterling as a reserve currency lingered on right into the negotiations about British entry into the European Community, when it was soon found that the issue did not exist.) It did not take long for Churchill's nightmare to come true: the United States, including the American dollar, took over the role which Britain had played in the past.

All this may sound like yet another story of decline. However, one can also look at it from a very different point of view. For one thing, the story shows Britain as a confident, understanding and far-sighted power, which does not try at a price to resist the drift of things, but accepts the spirit of the times, as Clement Attlee did when India became independent, and Harold Macmillan when he made his famous 'winds of change' speech about Africa. There was no British Captain Westerling who fought a lost battle for past glory (as happened to the Dutch in Indonesia), nor did Britain support a Tshombé out of naked self-interest (as did the Belgians in the Congo). Of course, Britain encountered difficulties on the way to becoming literally a little England; but on the whole, the country has mastered them well.

There emerged, from the debris of the Empire, a strange political creature called Commonwealth. The Commonwealth is one of those international entities which it is almost impossible to describe, except that it has a well-organised and brilliantly led secretariat, and arranges a Prime Ministers' conference every other year. It is the assembly of countries which regard Britain as their inspiration, accepted more or less grudgingly, but still accepted. It is also Britain's opportunity to help others, financially and commercially as well as culturally and at times politically. Its reality may be largely symbolic, but symbols can provide strong ties. Moreover, since no medium-sized country of Europe can discharge its responsibility to the poor countries by helping all of them, the Commonwealth is a useful grouping to concentrate such help, especially since with Canada, Australia and New Zealand, three other rich countries are among its members.

Post-Imperial Britain, then, is a country which shares some of the parameters of its international existence with other medium-sized powers in Europe, but in other respects is unique. Like France and Germany, Britain has to look on at the costly and deadly games which the new superpowers of the post-war world seem to enjoy playing. It can hope to be consulted, but it cannot hope to determine what happens. Like France, Britain resents this condition; more than France, it is forced into a position of impotence by its relative economic weakness. At the same time, the Imperial past has given Britain a rich treasure of experience, including experience in international responsibility. In one sense, it seems an accident today that Britain is one of the permanent members of the Security Council and Japan, say, is not; in another sense this is entirely appropriate. Britain can contribute to solving international problems by virtue of its historical role, and the wisdom which it conveys. Britain does not need to seek a place in international politics, for it already has one.

Chapter Nineteen
SPECIAL RELATIONSHIPS

There are four countries with which Britain enjoys, by virtue of its history and the ties which history has created, what might be called special relationships. This is most obviously the case with respect to Ireland; and here the notion that Britain *enjoys* a special relationship is also least appropriate. I have nothing to say about the Irish question that has not been said many times. It is an intractable question, or so it appears. One should have thought that for people in a civilised society, it is possible to live with heterogeneity. Somehow, our historical awareness suggests that while the Continental Thirty Years' War between Protestants and Catholics, from 1618 to 1648, was understandable, we have reached a level of sophistication today which should enable Protestants and Catholics to live, work, and run their affairs together. But if anything the opposite is the case. Not only do old conflicts linger on; but in the anomic world of modern societies the desire to be and remain among one's peers seems to have grown. Many people find it more rather than less difficult to accept difference. And so people try to sort themselves out, at a deadly price as the example of the Lebanon shows. In the process, the world becomes cruder and poorer, for accepting differences is both a symptom of civilisation and a stimulus to advance it.

Nowadays, the Irish question is linked up even with the original 'special relationship', that between Britain and its ancient colony, the United States of America. When Prince Charles went to New York to give the visit by the Royal Ballet his blessing, in 1981, both had a difficult time with Irish-American demonstrators who demanded 'political status' for the prisoners of the Maze prison. (A continental cannot but put 'political status' in quotation marks, because whoever has lived through a totalitarian regime knows that there is nothing worse than the invitation to arbitrary treatment implied by such status; in Nazi Germany in 1944, my father was safe once he got to a 'normal' prison in which clear and predictable rules were applied, and no longer had 'political status'.) The Irish-Americans also collect money to send arms to Northern Ireland and thus show that their loyalties are ethnic rather than national. But such incidents do not detract from the fact that there is a special relationship between Britain and America.

Again, the relationship is not easily described. It is both highly specific and very general. It is specific, for example, with respect to the MacMahon Rules which regulate the conditions under which Britain can develop its own nuclear deterrent. Under this agreement, Britain's nuclear force is not quite as independent as France's *force de frappe*; but no one in Britain seems to mind. For there is also the very general link between what are after all, all jokes to the contrary apart, English-speaking peoples. Was it Winston Churchill who said that the English and the Americans are two peoples divided by a common language? In fact, of course, the cultural bonds between the two countries continue to be important. It certainly was Churchill who, in his *History of the English-Speaking Peoples*, managed at the same time to understate and overstate the position when he said: 'The break between Britain and America made by the American Revolution was neither complete nor final.'[1]

For Britain, the history of Anglo-American relations has by no means been painless; yet on the whole the country has accepted its changing role with grace. Up to the First World War, Britain was unquestionably the senior partner in the relationship. But even before 1914, America had begun to emerge as a world power. Winston Churchill has described the battle for the union of the United States, the rise of the American economy, and then the process of gradually closing the open frontier. But 'with the process of settlement complete, and the work of economic development well in hand, [Americans] sought fresh fields in which to labour. By the 1890s the idea of Empire had taken hold of all the great industrial Powers. . . The European example was not lost upon America. For these and other reasons a vigorous spirit of self-assertion developed.'[2] Since 1900 or so, when it first appeared, that spirit has only intermittently left America. The First World War brought America's new role out into the open. Versailles was President Wilson's peace. In the inter-war years, it became increasingly clear that the roles of senior and junior partners had changed. Joseph Chamberlain had seen this process start many decades earlier; yet Neville Chamberlain in the 1930s tried briefly to arrest it. Appeasement was among other things an attempt to prevent the war which would finally put the seal on America's unrivalled power. But the war was not to be averted. The United States became the super-power which it is, and Britain became a junior partner in the alliance.

More recently, changes in American culture removed the country further from its traditional relationship. Affirmative action at last gave the American blacks a place in their country. Almost at the same time, America ceased to be the great melting-pot of immigrants from all over the world. People began to discover their 'ethnicity', that is, the national group to which they belonged. All of a sudden, it has become as important to be a Polish-American as it is to be an American. Then came the Hispanic immigration, and with it the first great challenge to the English language in the United States. Today, one would hesitate to speak of an 'English-speaking people'. And yet, through all these changes, and despite the hidden or open resistance by Britain to them, the relationship between the two countries has remained unique. British politicians, businessmen, and many others somehow have a special wire to their American counterparts. It is not forgotten that the two countries have a common history.

A common history also determines Britain's relations with France and Germany, though in these cases it is not only more turbulent and more recent, but above all incidental rather than necessary, a result of historical circumstances rather than a common heritage. This is why France and Germany could, and can, become the object of one of Britain's most charming vices, xenophobia. Not that France and Germany are simply disliked. There are many who love France, have a *gite* in the Dordogne, and go to spend their holidays there every year. Equally, there are many who love Germany, and they are not confined to the likes of Unity Mitford or even Christopher Isherwood. But strangely, love does not have to mean trust. There is a notable ambivalence about the attitudes of many Britons to the French and the Germans. There is also a notable absence of genuine understanding, including, of course, knowledge of the languages.

This is perhaps too strong a statement. It might be more correct to say that there are layers in the relationship between Britain and its European partners. But these layers present a mixed picture of closeness and distance. Take Germany. There is first of all, at least in the minds of many, Colditz, the battle between intelligent and good English officers and varied, but on the whole stupid and at any rate bad, German guards. Colditz casts the German 'in the role figure of the ridiculous or the dangerous alien'.[3] Karl Heinz Bohrer is not without comprehension for this attitude. He himself does not like the 'pompous, humourless, even authoritarian' style which is often ascribed to the Germans. The beer-swigging, noisy, earnest *kraut* in his *lederhosen* is actually hard to find in contemporary Germany, West or East; but his image abroad is nevertheless not easily dispelled. People are puzzled by German ways. Not that they always dislike them, but to many they seem odd and involuntarily funny, and at any rate very exotic. As a result there is a benevolent sense of puzzlement and surprise toward things German.

But of course this is only one layer of many in the complicated relationship between Britons and Germans. There is also the layer of official relations, which are good. At the regular meetings of heads of government and their ministers, the agenda contains few bilateral problems. Individual ministers get on with each other. There is, of course, the superiority of Britain as one of the four powers responsible for post-war Germany. Today this is epitomised above all by Britain's responsibility in Berlin. But this is easily compensated for by Germany's economic superiority. On the whole, a relaxed partnership has developed between the two countries, which belies the world of Colditz.

Then, at a somewhat deeper level, there is the admiration for German institutions. It is paradoxical in view of the history of the countries. Indeed, there are still Germans who would like to see British institutions, and the attitudes which go with them, transferred to the Continent. But today the opposite is equally widespread. Some examples have been quoted in earlier chapters. The Hansard Society Commission on Electoral Reform has recommended a variant of the German electoral system for Britain. The Bullock Committee of Enquiry on Industrial Democracy has borrowed heavily from the German experience of co-determination. This, of course, is often said to owe much to the influence of Britain as an occupation power, and notably to Ernest Bevin; but even so, it has become a German system. Lord Scarman in his Hamlyn Lectures bases much of his argument on what he calls the 'international challenge' which, in substance at least, is largely a French and a German challenge. The Committee to Review the Financial Institutions has found much to praise in the behaviour of German banks, as have Harold Lever and George Edwards in their articles. This list is far from complete. It demonstrates a reversal of institutional fortunes which again seems out of line with the Colditz attitude.

Economically, the envious glance at Germany is even more widespread. It does not always yield the same insights. Margaret Thatcher is impressed by the success of the market economy in Germany, whereas Shirley Williams is more interested in the experience of 'concerted action'. But all find the economic miracle of post-war Germany amazing, and would like to borrow a little from it. This is not so certain with respect to German attitudes. The man who beavers away from morning to night, has little time for the pleasures of life and always tries to outdo his peers, is an object of awe as well as admiration. One is impressed, though one does not want to be like him. The connection between economic success and attitudes to work and to life in general is not always made; naturally, many want to have their cake and eat it. In any case, the way Germans behave at work and in business relations takes one back full circle to Colditz. Quite a few Britons not only do not want to be like the Germans, but they do not like them.

Of course, all this reveals quite a lot about the British. It may well be just the situation which Bohrer puts in simple words: 'we are different from them, they are different from us.'[4] But he is a bit harsh when he explains English xenophobia in terms of economic decline: 'It is an ancient practice to project one's own difficulties to the outside. To find their own past impressive when their present is so frightening must be a temptation for the English. Thus historical nostalgia, chauvinism and cheap jokes at the expense of foreigners can all be explained by an instinct to survive without losing face. It has to be said again: England is a Narcissus who never tires of looking at himself in the mirror.'[5] If so, then the 'Narcissus' is harmless. There is nothing aggressive in the British way of maintaining difference. Some may feel offended by it, but if so, they probably suffer from wanting to be loved by all. After all, the British are different from the rest, and so are the rest from the British.

In any case, one should not exaggerate the importance of national attitudes. They always have many layers. A similar case to the one concerning Germany could undoubtedly be made for British attitudes to France and the French. There is the sneaking fondness for the way the French manage to enjoy life or are believed to do so; but then there is the suspicion that they are too clever by half and get the better of Britain in the European Community and elsewhere. One need not go on. The fact is that Britain, France and Germany are locked into a close relationship, and have been for some time. Today, this relationship is no longer one in which Britain can afford to ally itself with the weaker of the two (to whom of course Austria-Hungary and Russia would have to be added, if one talks about the old days) in order to maintain a 'balance of power' in Europe. Today, co-operation between the three is an inescapable prerequisite for maintaining some kind of world balance. Nor can such co-operation remain confined to the middle-sized powers of Europe. The Benelux countries and those of Scandinavia have their own role to play. Once again, the needs of the times are complex. Their complexity does not make it any easier to define one's identity. But difficult or not, there can be little doubt that Britain is today even more clearly what it has always been to a considerable extent, a European power.

Chapter Twenty

THE EUROPEAN DILEMMA

Clearly, Britain is a reluctant European. The ambivalence of many Britons to the French and the Germans is but a microcosm of a wider ambivalence towards the Continent. The Continent is of course called Europe in Britain; if one goes to Paris or Bonn one is going to Europe. Memories of the Empire and of the special relationship with the United States detract from Britain's European role. Unfortunately these memories were even more immediate when the foundations for the edifice of post-war Europe were laid, so that Britain sent its good wishes but was not a part of the process. To say that this is unfortunate is to take sides. But then it seems clear today that Britain's manifest destiny is European. There is no other place in which it can share sovereignty while maintaining its unique and rightly cherished traditions.

The story of Britain's relationship to the construction of Europe after 1945 is singularly unhappy. It is so unhappy that I almost called this chapter not 'The European Dilemma', but 'The European Calamity'. The story of Britain and Europe is calamitous. First, Britain was out when it should have been in; then, when Britain went in, it could well have afforded to stay out. This is an over-simplification, to be sure. It telescopes developments of which many are no longer aware. But it indicates in stark terms Britain's European dilemma. Perhaps there is a case for tracing the developments which have led to this predicament, however briefly, before the British position is assessed in somewhat greater detail.

The basis of what will continue here to be called the European construction in post-war Europe is a new relationship between France and Germany. It may be an overstatement, and even misleading, to speak of Franco-German friendship; a friendship does not need to be signed and sealed in the Cathedral of Reims as was the Franco-German Treaty in 1963, by de Gaulle and Adenauer. There were both a general and specific interests behind this new relationship. The general interest was one of putting an end to the internecine wars of a century and a half. The specific interests were more complicated. Germany had an interest in being welcomed back to the community of nations; and European co-operation seemed the most obvious means of achieving this end. France had an interest in tying Germany, one-half of the divided Germany, that is, firmly to an alliance, and given its national pride it preferred a European alliance. There may have been some asymmetry in these interests; but they were enough to get co-operation started, and once started new common interests rapidly developed.

Nevertheless, the start itself was halting, and peppered with failures. The Council of Europe soon turned out to be too weak an instrument to bring about the kind of co-operation that was required. France also overdid its interest game by making the Saar, temporarily separated from West Germany in 1946, a member; though French acceptance of the Saar referendum in 1955 marked an important step forward in the new Franco-German relationship. The Organization for European Economic Co-operation (OEEC) as it was then called, suffered from American membership, that is, from not being genuinely European. This, at any rate, was the French view. Then, the attempt to set up a European Defence Community (EDC) failed narrowly in the French parliament in 1954. The West European Union (WEU) had never been what its name suggests; it was set up to control German rearmament. Thus, by the mid-1950s the only effective European institution was the European Coal and Steel Community which had begun its work in 1952. It too suffered from the contrast between the political motives of its first President, Jean Monnet, and the manifest economic interests of its founders, and notably of France.

Thus, the Conference of Messina in 1955 was faced with a series of ruins of European integration, some still inhabited and some not, and the increasingly restrictive policies of European states, especially of France, so far as co-operation was concerned. The result was once again a hybrid, the European Economic Community. Its authors affirm in the preamble of the Treaty of Rome its political 'finalities', but they then proceed to contruct what is essentially an extended customs union. Indeed, they took up an old notion of the League of Nations, according to which a proper customs unions must not only harmonise tariffs, but also abolish non-tariff barriers and create common policies in areas in which member states did not rely on the market but allowed governments to interfere. Hence the common agricultural policy. But the important point to remember is that Article 235, which allows the member states to extend the activity of the EEC beyond the immediate objectives of the Treaty of Rome, has not, except by European zealots, been understood to be a *carte blanche* to turn the EEC into a political union. The EEC, and after the merger with the Coal and Steel Community and the Atomic Community in 1967, the European Communities (EC), are by the principles of their construction limited in scope. They fall far short of political union.

This is not to say that they were static constructions, set up once and for all with only decline and dissolution to look forward to. On the contrary, one of the strengths of the EEC was that it was a process both in time and in scope. Initially, it was the process of creating a customs union. In the years following its establishment in 1958, member states had an evident interest in free trade. The Kennedy Round at GATT which was to lower tariffs worldwide – and in which the EEC played an important and laudable role – was still some years hence. The Common Market was a desirable substitute for what was still missing in the world at large. Not surprisingly, trade between the original six members of the EEC increased rapidly. By the time the customs union was completed in 1970, they were interlinked to such an extent that separating them would have been terribly painful and was seen to be so.

Extension in scope meant several things. One was the much-maligned process of harmonisation. Its excesses, such as directives to have only one kind of bottle for beer, or to have all bread made of the same ingredients, have been the justified subject of laughter and of concern; but in essence, harmonisation means pulling down those barriers to trade which are other than tariffs. Extension in scope also involved a common agricultural policy (CAP). This is a complicated story, though one that had more plausibility than many Britons credit it with today. There was no market for agricultural products in the original member states of the EEC; almost all had government policies in this area. With some logic, it was decided therefore to have a common policy instead of a common market. This policy was then so designed that it would serve several quite different purposes at once, some of which were explicit, other implicit. Here is a fairly complete list of the objectives of the CAP: maintaining the income of farmers; making sure that the right mix of farm produce would be grown or bred; protecting internal prices by the equivalent of a tariff wall; cushioning adjustment, that is, cushioning the rapid reduction of the agricultural population; assuring a high degree of self-sufficiency. A formidable array of purposes! Moreover, some of these are clearly Continental and not British; the Continent never had to rely on convoys of threatened ships bringing food from distant places to the besieged island.

Of the main instrument that was chosen to achieve the objectives of the CAP, it may well be said that its application was too clever by half. For one instrument, prices, had to suffice to achieve a whole set of objectives. By fixing prices, farmers' incomes were guaranteed, a proper mix of products was brought about, external protection was achieved, and some of the other developments followed suit. Of course fixed prices had to be guaranteed. It is here that we get into the quagmire of the CAP; that is, its cost, and the system (if that is the word) of incomprehensible detail of regulations, directives and instructions. Until some years ago, it was said that there was one senior official of the Commission of the EEC who understood all this; but he has since retired. The cost of guaranteeing prices, even if more was produced than was needed, and of 'equalising' conditions all over the EEC, soon came to be the main issue. Since it had to be met, member states agreed to a system of 'own resources' of the EC (European Communities), accruing in part from customs and tariffs, and in part from a portion of VAT not exceeding 1 per cent of the total. This makes for a handsome income – in 1980, the Community's budget amounted to almost £10 billion – but more than 70 per cent of it was spent on the CAP. In fact, the European Communities are a customs union and an expensive agricultural policy, or at any rate this is what they were at the time of the Hague Summit of December, 1969.

This summit conference marks a turning point in the history of the European Communities. Since it, too, happened before Britain's entry – indeed, since it was the immediate cause of Britain's entry – it may again be useful to consider it briefly. The heads of government assembled at The Hague agreed on a programme of action which came to be couched in the form of a triptych, in French of course. The three wings of the piece of political art were: *achèvement, approfondissement, élargissement.*

Achèvement meant the achievement of the Common Market, that is, the full customs union of the Six. This was completed in the spring of 1970, once a few more agricultural regulations, including a disastrous one for the wine market, had been issued. But the achievement was in fact considerable. The common market boosted internal trade. The agricultural policy had made a mass exodus from the country bearable; the proportion of the population in farming had declined, throughout the Community, from 18 per cent in 1958 to 12 per cent in 1968; it has since declined further to 7 per cent. The Community had come to play a beneficial role in spreading free trade throughout the world. It had, as a separate policy, established helpful relations with a number of largely francophone developing countries under the Agreement of Yaoundé. It had elements of a research policy as a remnant of Euratom. It also had, largely as a latent instrument, what was left of the European Coal and Steel Community.

This is not a bad balance sheet of achievement. Yet there was a risk that with the *achèvement*, development would stop. The simile was used of the cyclist who falls off his bicycle if he stops pedalling. Where was the EC going to pedal to? The answer is provided by the dramatic, and in the end disastrous, story of the *approfondissement*, the attempted deepening of co-operation. Its theme was economic and monetary union. There were those who argued that if one has common agricultural prices, one must make sure that the currency in which they are expressed is controlled by the Community; for that reason, monetary union is indispensable. There were others who found further integration useful for political reasons, but insisted that monetary union should be preceded by economic union, that is, by common economic policies. A committee of the Council of Ministers under the chairmanship of the Prime Minister of Luxemburg, Pierre Werner, made proposals for moving towards monetary union. These were refined by the Commissioner responsible for Economic Policy and Finance, Raymond Barre (who was later to become French Prime Minister under President Giscard d'Estaing). In the end, in the spring of 1971, the Council of Ministers agreed on a 'plan in stages' towards economic and monetary union, and even decided to enter the first of its three stages which meant economic cooperation and a slight narrowing of the margins of fluctuation between the currencies of the member states. The third stage of full integration was to be reached within ten years.

However, this was not to be. In fact, it lasted only weeks before the realities of monetary developments swept away the great plans of the European Communities. First, floating started, and when European currencies were allowed to float, the decision to hold them together had become a scrap of waste paper. Then, on the 15 August, 1971, President Nixon gave notice to the monetary and trade systems of the post-war world by suspending the convertibility of the world's reserve currency, the dollar, into gold, and by imposing a surcharge on all imports into the United States. The surcharge was soon lifted, but Bretton Woods, the monetary arrangement to which the post-war world owes so much of its stability, was dented, if not destroyed for good. The effect on the European Community was traumatic. Despite a few imaginative attempts by Raymond Barre to save the plan, economic and monetary union was dead, never to be revived. The Community had to come to grips with the fact that it could no longer impose its own calendar on a recalcitrant world. It also had to accept that its most ambitious plans were out of tune with the times. Economic and monetary union would have meant political integration. This, however, could not only not be achieved in stages, as a customs union can; but it was in any case no longer in the obvious interests of the member states. Among other things, the floating of their currencies reminded them of their more immediate, and that means national, interests.

Thus, by 1972, the Community found itself naked. The older policies were still there; but new developments had been stunted. There was but one innovation, and that took place outside the Treaty of Rome, that is to say by inter-governmental co-operation. It, too, goes back to the Hague Summit at which a committee of high officials under the chairmanship of the then Secretary General of the Belgian Foreign Office, Vicomte Etienne Davignon (who later became a European Commissioner, responsible among other things for the European Coal and Steel Community), was set up to study possibilities of closer co-operation in matters of foreign policy. The result was the formalised system of Political Co-operation, involving regular meetings between foreign ministers and their political directors. This system has not led, and was not intended to lead, to binding decisions; but it has resulted in a growing convergence of foreign policy among members of the EC. But, to repeat the point, Political Co-operation is voluntary. It is not a part of the systematic arrangements of the European Communities.

In the absence of progress, the European Community turned to the third wing of the triptych, *élargissement*. This is of course where the British drama begins. It is not meant to be cynical if I say that Britain was rather like the young, idealistic suitor who was too enraptured to see the wrinkles in the face of his beloved; but the lady had a past, and worse, she suspected that the rejuvenation which she pretended to expect from the new courtship would turn out to be all but impossible. This is perhaps a little harsh to both sides. But there is an element of truth in the statement that whereas Britain entered the negotiations for entry with much of the idealism which had accompanied the early days of the EEC and its predecessors, the EC was already rather weary, and indeed worn. It was one of those clubs which had to offer little more than membership. It did not know where to go and therefore invited others, at best to a *Journey to an Unknown Destination* (as Andrew Shonfield's important 1972 Reith Lectures on Europe were called[1]), at worst to the boredom of administering the past which was not that of new members.

This was made worse by the fact that the past of the European Economic Community had little relevance for Britain. The common agricultural policy ran counter to a century of different developments in Britain. It meant that food had to become more expensive, though perhaps the changes in so-called world market prices which have happened since Britain's entry are not always fully appreciated. Moreover, Britain joined the customs union at a time when trade was slackening generally. After August 1971 and the Yom Kippur War just over two years later, the order of the day was not expansion, but contraction, or at any rate stabilisation. Moreover, the Common Market operated like all markets: it strengthened the strong and weakened the weak. There is no doubt that overall Germany has benefited more from the enlarged Common Market than Britain, though there is equally no doubt that if Britain wants to recover its economic strength it needs, among other things, larger markets. All this adds up to one clear conclusion: Britain entered the European Community too late, and when it entered, it was the wrong Community for Britain.

But clearly this is not all there is to be said on the subject. There is in fact no place for Britain in the world other than Europe. The Commonwealth and the special relationship with America add a special touch, and an implication of wider obligations, to Britain's identity, but they do not detract from the need to find its role in European co-operation. When Britain realized this fact – and it is probably right to assume that the European referendum of 1975 was a vote for this recognition rather than for the Common Market and the CAP – there was only one Europe available, and that was the Europe of the European

Communities. One hopes that, if contemporaries do not, historians will agree that it is to the lasting credit of Edward Heath as Prime Minister to have swallowed the many reservations which he undoubtedly had, and to have taken the leap which was necessary for Britain to find its identity as a European country.

In the first instance, to be sure, the leap has led to doubts rather than to certainties. Most people in Britain regard the European Community as costly in more ways than one, as a source of absurd policies, and in any case as one of those foreign contraptions which destroy what is dear to Britain. They are wrong. The cost of the Community is vastly exaggerated in the minds of many; even before any alleviation, Britain's net payments amounted to no more than just over £1 billion, that is, government income from about fifty day's production of North Sea oil. This has now been reduced to about one-third of these figures, or even less, according to recent data. For a central plank of foreign policy, this is not a high price, though the Community would be well advised to adjust it to the economic strength of its members. The policies of the Community are a result of shared sovereignty; there is no need for Britain to accept patent nonsense. Moreover, there are EC policies of which one can be proud. The agreement of Yaoundé has been replaced, in the Community of Nine, and now Ten, by two successive Agreements of Lomé which cover 61 developing countries and are a model of responsibility for the Third World. The beginnings of a regional and a social policy, both actually leftovers of the abortive attempt at creating economic and monetary union which they were supposed to prop up, make sense for Britain. Agricultural products are no longer cheap anywhere. The common market has proved adaptable, some would say too adaptable, to the requirements of those who do not benefit obviously from its openness.

Moreover, there is progress. It has taken place outside the framework of the Treaty of Rome and the other Treaties and does not yet have the binding quality of Community decisions; but in order to be a part of it at all, one has to be a member of the Community. This is true for Political Co-operation in which Britain has come to play an important role, if not one of leadership. Co-operation in foreign policy is a necessary condition of world influence at a time when superpowers dominate the field. New opportunities have also been offered by the European Monetary System (EMS) which, contrary to its name, is a flexible and essentially voluntary arrangement which may well have its uses for

Britain. There are other developments, such as the European Science Foundation in which the research councils and academies of a larger Europe co-operate. All these and others offer opportunities of sharing sovereignty and of gaining influence by it, and Britain would be the poorer if it was not a part of them.

This difficult and to some extent painful story requires one footnote before it can be drawn to a conclusion. It has to do with the relative importance of Europe, and more particularly of the European Communities, in the context of Britain's foreign policy. This importance has been inflated beyond belief in public debate in Britain. There were those who had hoped that the Community would turn Britain overnight into a super-power, or at least a critical part of one; but such Imperial dreams were always misguided. If anything, the Community is strong and respected because it is *not* a superpower. Then there were, and are, those who believe that everything that has gone wrong in Britain since it became a member of the EC on January 1973, has its origins in Brussels; but such conspiracy theories were also always misguided. The Community does not account for the major part of Britain's economy at all; in any case, the story of Britain's decline is very much longer than that of its involvement with Europe. The Community does not account, either, for the major part of Britain's overall policies, nor is it likely to do so in future; if one could quantify its importance, one would not be likely to assess it as determining more than 5 per cent of Britain's overall political interest, and the estimate may well be on the high side. Thus, the enormous fuss that is made in Britain by supporters and opponents of 'Europe' is in part a curious distraction, far removed from the realities of politics and of economic life. '*Niedriger hängen!*' Frederick the Great of Prussia is supposed to have said when he saw the portrait of a man for whom he had little time hanging on a wall somewhere. 'Hang it lower!' would not be bad advice for Britain's public attitude to the European Communities.

What, then, is the balance of the argument? First of all, it is that Britain would be ill-advised to leave the European Community, however tempting this might be for those who do not wish to explain decline in terms of their own failures. Economic and political isolation are a recipe for impoverishment and impotence. The arguments advanced against protectionism apply to the European Communities with even greater force. Even those who are far away from Europe, including the United States and many Commonwealth countries, find it difficult to understand why Britain keeps dithering about where it belongs. They prefer to deal with a reasonably compact Community. An insulated medium-sized power is more pathetic than impressive these days.

Secondly, it is certainly right that Britain should try to change the Community's ways. The system of own resources is not adequately related to the expenditure of the EC; either one or the other, or both, will have to be changed. Once the Community reaches the ceiling of income agreed by the member states, that is, tariff income and 1 per cent of VAT, the need for such changes will be evident. But no-one should have any illusions about these reforms. The Community is a customs union plus a common agricultural policy, and that it will remain. Vested interests in important member states are too strong to allow significant change. Whatever happens by way of reform will therefore inevitably be patchwork. Reform of the Community cannot sensibly be the main objective of a country which takes Europe seriously.

This main objective has to be linked to the new developments which have already taken place at the margin of the European Communities. Political Co-operation and the European Monetary System are only a beginning. The German Foreign Minister, Hans-Dietrich Genscher, has proposed a series of steps which would lead to a European Union taken seriously. European Union still means shared sovereignty, and not the creation of a new European super-state. It is the kind of objective which could see Britain as a driving force. Accepting the comparative irrelevance of the Communities as they are, and concentrating on new developments by its members, is the real task of anyone who regards Europe as a force for the good in the world.

Even so, it is important for Britain not to lose its sense of perspective so far as Europe is concerned. In the other member states of the Community, Europe has already found its place, important, but not all-important. Britain is a European country. It is therefore right that it should be an active contributor to the European construction. But Britain must play this role in full awareness of the fact that Europe is not its only source of a national identity. Britain documents by its interests the complexity with which mature nations can live, and all nations have to learn to live. It might well be a confident island, unworried about sharing its sovereignty with others in contexts which add to its influence, firmly based in Europe but wide open to other, older relations. Britain might be a model for the world.

A FUTURE THAT MIGHT WORK

Chapter Twenty-one
BRITAIN IN THE 1980s

The condition of Britain in the 1980s is rather less than wholesome. Even a benevolent analysis of the state of the country cannot but conclude that there are serious problems. The notable strengths of British politics and society were always ambiguous, but now they have come to be eroded. The static class system, arranged like a layer cake, has helped the country avoid the restlessness of others; it has also damped down all attempts at improving productivity and with it, prosperity. Britain's unique mixture of adversary politics and a corporate bias has given much enjoyment to the players, if not the spectators, and from time to time it has even worked; but by preventing a clear option for either it has failed to bring about the necessary consensus of important groups. Britain's identity as a country has more to go on than other countries of comparable size can claim; but the very diversity of options has made it difficult for the country to know where to go. There are other ways of describing these ambiguous strengths. Continuity, excellence, liberty and solidarity were the concepts which were used in introducing the theme of this book. But there is no denying, as a conclusion approaches, that the precarious balance between strengths and weaknesses is broken. Today, it is a memory more than a reality. The reason is that the strengths themselves have begun to falter. As a result Britain is now faced with two issues to which there are no easy answers: that of maintaining a viable economic base, and that of preserving social cohesion.

So far as the economic base is concerned, things have gone from bad to worse. One must wonder whether the word, recession, which is so often used to 'explain' Britain's economic condition, is not misleading. Is one really talking about a patch of bad weather which has reached

Britain's shores from somewhere else – or is Britain's climate in fact more insular, is it home-made? The economic problem is not only the absolute decline which has set in in the 1960s; it is what has come to be called 'de-industrialization', that is, the erosion of the manufacturing base. In the 1970s, Britain's gnp still rose by several percentage points (though it began to decline after 1979), but manufacturing output declined in absolute terms. Nor is this a short-term process. Whereas in Germany, employment in industry accounts for 45 per cent of total employment, the corresponding percentage for Britain is just over 30 per cent. The fact that there are manufacturing industries which continue to do well, does not detract from the overall picture. British Leyland is more than merely a symptom of general trends. After all, the automobile industry is still said to be the engine of the rest. Directly and indirectly, its effect on employment and output is great. Yet in Britain, this engine has been stuttering for many years; and today it works at the most on three of its four cylinders. The automobile industry may not keep its position for much longer; but there is not much sign of possible future engines of industry, such as electronics, being much stronger in Britain. This is, of course, only a part of the economic story. Manufacturing is not everything; indeed, as we shall see, the advocates of a 'post-industrial society' believe that its importance is declining. Even growth is not everything. Yet de-industrialisation is not to be taken lightly.

This is especially true if we put it in a wider economic context which is one of disappointments and frustrations. Take North Sea oil. Many had hoped that the decades in which North Sea oil was available would help re-industrialise Britain, and generally bolster its economy. Either the resulting self-sufficiency in energy, or Government income from North Sea oil and its possible uses, or indeed the fact that there was at least one highly prosperous and dynamic industry, was considered by many to be a source of general improvement. But the many were wrong. One is tempted to say that they were obviously wrong. Self-sufficiency is of little use if imported energy is no more expensive than domestic energy; British industry has not been given more favourable prices. Government income from North Sea oil is, as such, of little use. Even if it were to be used for gigantic projects it would probably do little more than it does at the moment (though it might do it in a more decent manner): it would finance the unemployed. Whereas now this is done by unemployment benefits to the tune of just about the annual public income from oil, it would then be done by putting people on pay-rolls which would probably not be much more productive than those of local government. Many experts believe, for good reason, that these days money is the least obstacle in the way of economic development. Where there are viable projects, the will to move forward and the readiness to work hard, money will come almost by itself. The availability of money, on the other hand, does not create the will to grow. It may even do the opposite. North Sea oil is in a sense a new Empire, found at the bottom of the sea; it makes an effort unnecessary and serves to confirm the tired structures which exist. Oil is therefore not an engine which moves the rest of industry ahead.

Thus, Britain's economic condition has to be described in stark and unpleasant terms. Economic decline has reached the point at which it is no longer possible to distinguish between the condition of the country and that of individuals. Britain finds it difficult to maintain, let alone to expand, its gross national product. While wages may still rise, such increases are largely eaten up by inflation. In any case, if they continue to rise for those at work, the prosperity of the employed is paid for by the unemployed, whose numbers have reached three million. People's reaction to this condition varies. Some have work and the clout, or the ability, to improve their position. They will do well, especially by comparison to the rest. Some despair and leave the country. They find work in other countries where they feel that their efforts are rewarded, and above all that making an effort is not antisocial behaviour. Some get along by earning enough in the black economy. They work long hours, but come home with bundles of £10 and £20 notes which they use to improve their homes and their cars, or to go on holidays abroad. Some sink into the underclass. While this leaves the majority in a bearable position, it describes a situation in which everybody fends for himself, not one of general progress, or even of holding the fort. It must be said in all brutality: there is no indication whatsoever of unemployment being reduced significantly, inflation abating seriously, and above all of the economy of Britain returning to the growth trail. Britain not only shares the condition of the rest of the OECD world, which is one of considerable difficulties in the face of economic growth, but it has eroded its own potential for improvement to a frightening extent. There is little or no chance of Britain being significantly better off at the end of the century than it was in the 1960s, and a good chance that the country as a whole, and many individuals in it, will be worse off.

All this occurs at a time at which the greatest strength of the country, its voluntary cohesion, its civic virtues, its sense of solidarity, are under stress. Some argue that economic and civic decline are related; they would like to explain riots and crime entirely in terms of poverty and unemployment. The connection is probably more tenuous, and more indirect. While unemployment tears the social fabric apart, the recreation of full employment would not by itself rebuild it. While poverty, and the existence of an underclass of considerable magnitude, make a mockery of solidarity and other civic virtues, these virtues do not suffice to solve the problem, nor does solving the problem of itself lead to the re-constitution of self-discipline and cohesion by choice rather than by force. In any case, there are other reasons for the breakdown of cohesion. Some have already been listed: the challenge of race, the loneliness of youth, the decline of the old middle classes, if not of all three old classes, the general disruption of social ligatures. The latter at least has happened elsewhere as well. Indeed, perhaps Britain is merely joining the rest, if it replaces a self-sustaining system of getting on with others by what some call *anomie*, that is, the absence of binding rules of behaviour.

This is no consolation. It is never a consolation to join others in misery, however cosy it may feel to be in company. Britain in particular has reason to be proud of its very special virtues. If the cohesion of a society is based on crude power, and this power for some reason lapses, then there are ways of re-establishing it. One can always call in the police if one has relied on them throughout. This is what most Continental countries do. But calling in the police is not a British answer; at any rate, it was not an answer in the past. If a self-sustaining system of social control, that is, the unforced kindness of people to each other, breaks down, one is left with a vacuum which is not easily filled. The temptation will be to substitute crude power for more subtle rule by agreement. Under such conditions, one is quite likely to see nasty incidents involving the police as well as violent action against them.

In these circumstances, the call for 'law and order' is widespread. It is understandable, though it has been abused. It also promises the wrong remedy. Abuses arise above all from a mechanical understanding of what order means, a police notion or order. The ultimate order of a cemetery is as frightening as the orderly marching columns of a Nazi Party Congress. Law and order is the wrong remedy because of the manner in which it invokes the law. In Britain, at least, there is a very different tradition of social cohesion. Contrary to the United States – a notoriously violent country – and to the countries of Continental Europe – traditionally relying on state power – British life has never been 'legalised'. In Britain, the rule of law is not the rule of lawyers or even of judges. Britain is neither a litigious society in which individuals and groups fight out their battles by calling on the courts, nor is it a state society in which the courts are used as instruments of explicit domination. This is, or was, a strength of British society. If all rules have to be made explicit, and all conflicts resolved by reference to explicit rules, there is likely to be a breakdown of trust, of spontaneous relations between people, and, of course, of self-sustaining cohesion. Where there is liberty, the law is always the second best instrument for defending it; where it becomes the best, indeed the only, one, liberty is often under threat.

Yet re-building a society in which people live together without invoking police and the law at every other step they take, is a long and difficult process. Perhaps re-building is the wrong word in any case. One cannot build social ligatures like a high-rise block, or even like an equal-opportunities code. They have to grow, and such growth can take decades. Perhaps one can create conditions under which their growth is more likely than under others. For example, abstaining from bringing more and more activities within the orbit of the state is a condition of liberty and of self-discipline, even if at times such abstinence has consequences which worry those in power. Linkages and self-discipline grow more easily in a market society than in a state society. But the necessary condition is by no means a sufficient condition. This is why Britain's tradition of civic virtues and solidarity is so precious. This is also why the partial breakdown of the tradition is so serious.

The two problems of economic decline and social anomie, related and yet separate, add up to a formidable set of concerns. One can understand why a mood of gloom and a sense of hopelessness have become so widespread in Britain that one can almost speak of a clinical depression of the British public. The rare bouts of mania by which it is punctuated not only do not last, but are indeed manic, that is, wild fantasies of ultimate solutions. The British like the idiosyncratic; so they fall for patent solutions. But of course such lapses are invariably followed by even deeper depressions. Not even attempts to shake the country out of its gloom by painting its condition in the blackest terms promise much success. James Bellini's *Rule Britannia*, which the author calls 'a progress report for Domesday 1986' is such an attempt. '"Rule

Britannia! . . . Britons never, never shall be slaves." One day, if the conditions of everyday life continue to be eroded by failing industry and glaring inequalities, they may decide that the impossible has happened.'[1] But the readers are not shocked. They are in any case no longer expecting anything better. They even get, to paraphrase the (German) title of Karl Heinz Bohrers' book on Britain, 'a little frisson out of decline'.[2]

Let me leave no doubt: in my view this just will not do. It may well be that the world is doomed to the prospect of nuclear disaster, or that the developed world is heading for a long period of economic decline and socio-political instability, or that Britain will not be able to cope with its two great problems – but first of all, we do not know whether these prospects will become real, and secondly, even if we did, it would be small-minded and above all faint-hearted to sit back in the face of such threats and just moan and groan. Surely, if things look bad, one has to do something about them. Something is not just anything, to be sure. Blind splurges are in fact the preference of those who don't care, who have given up. One has to do something effective, something that goes to the root of the problems and makes use of the instruments which one has got, rather than of imaginary tools which someone thinks are ideal. Britain is so strong at its social core – surely it must be possible to apply this strength to its economic, political, and more general social problems.

Chapter Twenty-two
MODELS OF BRITAIN

Fortunately, not everybody in Britain wallows in gloom. Politicians in particular are forced by the requirements of their profession to think about what to do in order to take the country into a better future. As a result, Britain has a surprising number if not of philosopher-kings then of author-politicians. The latter are in any case more welcome in a free society than the former. By author-politicians, I do not mean the growing number of those who have given professors of politics many academic years worth of teaching material through their diaries and memoirs; though it might just be mentioned in passing that interest in the intestines of the political process is a very British pastime, for in most countries the equivalent of the *Crossman Diaries* would sell at most two thousand copies. But what is meant here is the attempt by those who are in the middle of the fray, or who wait for their moment of action, to sketch their ideas for the future of Britain. It is worth looking at some of their suggestions before turning to the concluding argument of this book which attempts to translate the analyses of earlier chapters into prescription, or at any rate into perspectives for change.

Needless to say, few author-politicians defend things as they are, or even advance the traditional philosophies of their parties. Those who believe that one can build on the past and its strengths are more likely to be actors than authors. Ian Gilmour is an exception in this as in other respects. His pamphlet, *Inside Right. A Study of Conservatism*[1] as well as a number of his speeches, are a considered an important attempt to apply Disraeli's belief in 'one nation' and the Conservatist insistence on the traditional strengths of Britain to the problems of the day. On the Labour side, a similarly traditional approach is advanced by the authors of *Crosland's Legacy* (which is misleadingly called, *The Socialist*

Agenda, for the approach is avowedly social democratic); though of them, only Giles Radice and Lord Donaldson can be described as active politicians. Starting point of the volume is the traditionalist, not to say conservative belief that Crosland's 'brand of radical humanitarianism, his creed of equality with liberty, still contain the seeds of a rich harvest'.[2]

However, the prevailing approach to political theory is a very different one. Many would agree with the author-politician who considers past economic and social developments and the possibility of continuing along the same lines, only to find: 'The necessary conclusion for anyone giving calm consideration to the range of alternative futures theoretically available to the people of this country is that this one, based upon a fond nostalgia for the 1950s and 1960s, ought no longer to be a serious runner.' There are, in the view of this author, three major reasons why this should be so: the fear that going on as in the past 'may put at risk our particular form of liberal representative democracy', the fact that 'British society . . . is changing in any case in directions which will not permit us to [go on as we have been], even though many of us may wish to do so', and 'the pace and direction of technological change' which is bound to involve a transformation of the economy.[3] Not all may agree with these reasons; but there are at least three, if not four schools of political thought in Britain today which start with the need for fundamental change.

The first of these is Conservative. Indeed, strange as this may sound, the MP whose demand for change we have quoted is Nigel Forman, Conservative MP for Carshalton. However, Nigel Forman probably does not agree with the new conservatism which has come to such prominence in recent years. Actually, there is nothing conservative about it except the capital C. Starting point of this radical policy of the right is the desire to lead Britain out of the economic and social malaise of recent decades. With this intention, there would be little disagreement; but the diagnosis offered by the new Conservatives is peculiar. In essence it aims at reviving, or perhaps bringing to life for the first time in Britain, a market economy. This requires quenching the inflationary virus, but above all creating a world of incentives instead of safeguards, of carrot-and-stick rather than of the cushioned life of the welfare state. There is much of *The Future That Doesn't Work* in this diagnosis. So far as the remedy is concerned, it can be ascribed to three names: Milton Friedman, Arthur Laffer, Friedrich von Hayek.

Milton Friedman and his theory of inflation marks, as it were, the first step of the process. If one succeeds – so the argument runs – in controlling the money supply effectively over a period, then inflation is bound to go down to near zero. Once inflation is reduced to this level, one important precondition of reliable growth has been created. It is not altogether clear what is meant by money supply here, at least for practical purposes. There is also the dilemma of the length of time it takes to show results – two years? three years? – and the need for early political success. Moreover, controlling the money supply has a price, such as high interest rates and their effect on credit. The cure may kill the patient before the conditions for rejuvenation are created. But the theoretical point is clear.

The second stage of the process has come to be associated with Arthur Laffer, the American economist whose curve, the 'Laffer curve', is so beautifully simple that politicians understand it. Laffer's curve relates tax rates to government revenues and shows that once tax rates exceed a certain level, revenues actually decline. In turn, this means that lowering tax rates may increase revenues if one has passed the magic point at which more means less. This is so not only because people are more honest, but above all because more is earned if lower taxes provide incentives. Thus, in Britain – and according to the new Conservatism – taxes have to be lowered. Again, there is no telling where exactly the turning point lies. Moreover, stipulating an incentive effect of tax cuts means making assumptions about people's behaviour which are not necessarily correct.

Underlying all this there is a philosophical conviction which has to do with equality, and which Friedrich von Hayek has consistently coupled with monetarism and the demand for incentives. Keith Joseph and Jonathan Sumption acknowledge their debt to Hayek in their book entitled *Equality*. The book should have been called 'Inequality', because its point is to 'challenge one of the central prejudices of modern British politics, the belief that it is a proper function of the State to influence the distribution of wealth for its own sake'.[4] For the authors, one of whom is after all a senior British politician, equality is the British disease. By breaking down class barriers, equality has made people more envious without making them more productive. In the process, fundamental requirements of individual welfare and social progress have been forgotten. 'Ultimately the capacity of any society to look after its poor is dependent on the total amount of its wealth, however distributed.'[5] The total amount of wealth can be increased only if inequality is permitted, indeed if it is actively encouraged. 'The speed of a society's advance is the speed of its fastest members, and a society in which no one may advance an inch before another will remain immobile.'[6]

The striking feature of this entire theory is how little it has to go on in the British tradition. It is a deliberate and radical break with that tradition. Even 'Manchester liberalism' was more compassionate, more oriented to the tradition of solidarity. Indeed, if there is any real example of the Friedman-Laffer-Hayek theory in operation, it is the United States of America. The Federal Republic of Germany was in fact always a consensus country in which Ludwig Erhard represented but one, if a crucial, element. It is only in America that supply-side economics is in line with people's behaviour, that is to say, that tax reductions are likely to lead to higher investment rather than higher consumption. In combination with the evident cost in terms of unemployment, bankruptcies and decline, it is the cultural alienness of this approach which is most likely to defeat it. Moreover, its practical failure and the tradition of values in which it is tried, are related. There is every sign that the new Conservative theory will have a short life in political practice.

The counterpart of this theory on the left, which is represented most explicitly by Tony Benn, has quite different heroes. Keith Joseph is probably right when he argues that British egalitarianism is based not so much on Marx as on Rousseau, that it is 'of the romantic rather than the intellectual kind'[7]; but Tony Benn insists that his approach, which he calls 'democratic socialism', is 'very much a home-grown British product which has been slowly fashioned over the centuries'.[8] Not all its antecedents are purely British; Benn likes to invoke the Bible, and, in a slightly roundabout way, Marx; but the Levellers, the Chartists and the Fabians certainly are British. Certain words recur in Tony Benn's political vocabulary. They include 'equality'; 'brotherhood'; 'sharing' all manner of things and notably 'power'; 'rank and file'; 'the people'; 'the working people'. Apart from this egalitarian language, there is the pride of the many as expressed by the word 'sovereignty', and the nationalism which pervades Benn's speeches and writings. When he extols the virtue of 'British socialism', he sees it as 'drawing its inspiration from many sources and absorbing them all into a belief in basic human equality and freedom, to be expressed in the democratic forms of chapel, union and Parliament, to which all power should be accountable'.[9]

Industry and the economy figure greatly in Tony Benn's thinking. Indeed, his approach is almost totally production-oriented, and thus among other things in the ascetic tradition of British socialism. In its orientation to production, the approach involves a deep contradiction.On the one hand, Tony Benn seeks ways of central planning and organisation. In his view, the main reason for Britain's poor economic performance is the weakness of the 'mixed economy'. This has to be replaced by public ownership, and by planning agreements, indeed by a 'National Plan'. Such a National Plan will be developed and implemented by leaders who are accountable to the people; it will therefore deal with the real issues of jobs, wages and production rather than with profits.

On the other hand, Tony Benn never forgets the essential purpose of his reforms, that is, 'a shift in the balance of power and wealth'.[10] 'We are not interested in ownership just for the sake of ownership. We are concerned with the power that ownership carries with it to shape our future.'[11] This means that state ownership is not the answer. Tony Benn clearly likes 'work-ins', 'workers' co-operatives', and generally the decentralisation of power and authority. That is to say, he likes it within limits. His arguments about decentralisation and the necessary power of trade unions are perhaps a little contorted. Above all, his discussion of nuclear energy betrays the extent to which he is torn between fascination for the centralised use of technology and a belief in the need to listen to the people wherever they work and live. From his presentation of 'The Debate over Nuclear Energy', one must gather two things: the fact that technology is crucially important; and the belief that people's views are crucially important. It is too bad that people's views are out of step with technological possibilities. 'The question is not whether these [views of people] are valid points because, of course, they are valid points. The question is whether they are so decisive as to justify overturning the basic energy policy, with all its risks.'[12]

Tony Benn himself distinguishes between 'monetarism', 'corporatism', and 'democratic socialism' as political alternatives. The list is incomplete, but not without meaning. Benn's democratic socialism is about a shift of power to 'the people'. Wherever possible, he wants the people to exercise power at their workplace. It is no accident that in his list of 'democratic forms', the chapel comes before the union, and the union before Parliament. But Benn knows that a modern industrial society needs larger units, and a central decision-making apparatus. Much of the shift of power with which he is concerned has to do therefore with the accountability of a more open government which would have a responsibility that is unheard of in free societies. Whatever Benn may say about leaders who are not noticed because they have created 'the conditions that will allow the people to do it themselves',[13] in the real world this is bound to mean that leaders do not allow protest because they have decreed the happiness of the people. There is no example of a centrally planned 'managed economy', doing anywhere near as well as a market economy, nor has the kind of democratisation which Benn advocates ever meant anything other than the rule of a minority of activists over an impotent majority. Thus the practice of this theory is likely to look much less benevolent than the theory itself. Yet there is something in Benn's approach which does in fact follow the British tradition, and which may therefore yet win the day.

One of the reasons why Benn's list of political approaches is incomplete is that he has underestimated the new Social Democrats. The term 'social democrats' is a little misleading. Those who call themselves SDP may well agree in important respects with the authors of Emmett Tyrell's book on *Social Democracy's Failures in Britain*; they might even share Tony Benn's view that 'the one solution that no longer seems to be on offer is social democracy', at any rate if it is defined as 'the philosophy which has dominated the last thirty years or so'.[14] But they believe that there is a new kind of social democracy. Its main advocates among those who are both political actors and authors are David Owen with his book *Face the Future*, and Shirley Williams and her *Politics Is For People*. Both David Owen and Shirley Williams believe that prevailing political analyses remain superficial. The first sentence of Owen's book is: 'Let us face facts: The British nation has been ill served by its political parties over the last quarter of a century.'[15] Shirley Williams dismisses explanations of economic decline as they underly the thinking of the right and the left, and concludes that the 'changes we are seeing . . . are not temporary. Nor are they simply the product of past policy mistakes, though these have made their contribution. They cannot even be attributed to one system, capitalist or communist, for both systems are visibly cracking under the stress. The crisis is a crisis of industrialism itself.'[16]

It is characteristic of the social democrats that they combine this kind of radical analysis with gradualist proposals for change. They believe in 'piecemeal engineering' as Karl Popper has described it; indeed their commitment to the open society, their abhorrence of dogmatism, in this sense their belief in democracy, is the main reason why they have set up a new party at all. So far as the direction of reform is concerned, David Owen has made his most original contribution with respect to the political principle of decentralisation, and Shirley Williams in the chapters on the nature of the future economy.

The starting point of David Owen's argument about political institutions sounds almost like a straight quote from Keith Middlemas: 'Corporatism is a recipe for choosing the lowest common denominator, for the stifling of initiative and innovation.'[17] Owen believes that the corporate bias is one of the main sources of the absence of necessary changes. He holds against this bias the need for an 'extension of democracy' which can be satisfied by remembering 'the de-centralist tradition' of political, and notably of socialist, thought. Owen advocates all the safeguards of political democracy, such as more open government, electoral reform, two chambers, and the like, but his central thesis is that we need 'a rethink of political attitudes towards centralisation and decentralisation'.[18] This would be in line not only with the tradition of political thought but also with that of political reality. Devolution responds to the desires of the nations of Britain. Stronger local government can build on 'the great cultural traditions of cities like Manchester, the strengths of provincial England': 'The time is overdue for a reassertion of a different balance where local government recovers some of its former powers and influence and where a more variegated pattern of government matches the rich cultural distinctions between Devon and Derbyshire, Leeds and Bristol.'[19] Nor does decentralisation have to be confined to political administration in the narrow sense; the welfare state could and should be dissolved into a system of community care. There remains an important role for central government, but decentralisation is the order of the day.

Shirley Williams adds her own illustrations to this approach. She even sees a connection between new technologies, which play a major part in her argument, and decentralisation. Through microprocessors, 'the decentralisation of work and decision-making ceases to be a dream'. More than that, 'human beings can be made whole again, working and living in the same community.'[20] As David Owen advocates what he calls 'freedom with security', that is, law and order by self-discipline, so Shirley Williams insists that 'the quality of life . . . is made not only out of a widening of opportunities, but also out of a sense of belonging, of being cared for, of being wanted, of being part of a network of relationships with people and also with objects.'[21] Where the new conservatism advocates an individualist world of competition and success or failure, and the new left the brotherhood of equals, social democrats seeks the fraternity of people who in the real world are likely to be unequal in their position and different as individuals, but who can live together.

Capitalism and communism have failed, corporatism is not the answer, technology and society have changed, but work in the sense of jobs for all remains a personal and social necessity – this is not exactly an easy bundle of assumptions on which to build an economic policy. Shirley Williams gears her proposals very largely to employment. 'Reversing the tide of concentration' in industry means that small and medium-sized firms offer more jobs.[22] Accepting technological change means not only that work can be done at home, but also that new jobs are created ('vacancies for computer programmers, systems analysts, electronic technicians and design engineers are hard to fill . . .'[23]). 'An ordered transition from school to work for all young people' would involve a trainee or apprenticeship scheme and deal with youth employment[24]. There can, and should be changes in the duration and structure of working lives. Job creation makes sense in areas in which otherwise nothing would be done, 'ranging from afforestation and the clearing of rivers and canals to improving derelict neighbourhoods or insulating existing housing stocks'.[25] All this serves both social and individual purposes; it is designed to improve the quality of life. Shirley Williams takes up the tradition of Tawney and others: 'We have been mesmerised into using the productivity of labour as the most important criterion of economic achievement.'[26] A new attitude can create a new society which is economically viable and makes people happier.

The social democratic image of society is humane and liberal. It presupposes democratic institutions which are strengthened in a variety of ways. It aims at building political and economic change around smaller units. It seeks the removal of barriers to a society of more evenly spread opportunities without ever confusing this with equality of results. It emphasises the quality of life rather than the quantity of production. It sees countries embedded in a wider international context from which they benefit and to which they contribute. All this is to be achieved as much by changes in attitudes as by institutional reform. In short, this view represents the best of the society which in most countries is called 'industrial'. It is a reasonable view, indeed, if anything, one which is too reasonable in view of the profound quality of the changes which are taking place and the frightening nature of the threats to survival of justice and liberty today.

Liberals share many views with Social Democrats. This is above all the case with respect to institutional reforms. There are differences also; Liberals have in some ways become an extra-parliamentary party which is not excessively eager for power in central government. In community politics, they have many an achievement, and in any case a lively interest to their credit. Also, they canalise anti-Westminster sentiment in a rather effective manner. Yet a tactical coalition with the Social Democrats is in the obvious interests of both. It might well change the face of British politics, at least for a while. One general election won by the alliance, or even a hung parliament, would make a big difference in institutional terms. The alliance might not last, and its constituent parties might not find it so easy to cope with the future; but the foundations of British politics would have been changed.

For in Britain, voters have in principle four alternatives today. One is the traditional conservative attitude of trying to build on Britain's strength and muddling through. It was last represented by James Callaghan as Prime Minister. After him, no obvious representative of this approach has emerged in any party. A second is the experiment of the Friedman-Laffer-Hayek right. It has been tried, and will probably not be tried again very soon. The third is the experiment of the left, that is, the middle-class socialism of Tony Benn. It appeals to certain British traditions while at the same time offering power to the hitherto disenfranchised educational class and its allies. It is probably true to say that like the radicalism of the right it has one chance, no more. If it does not succeed soon, it will slip into a permanent minority position. Whether it succeeds or not, depends to a large extent on the fourth alternative, the Liberal-Social Democratic alliance.

The most striking feature of this is the missing fifth alternative. In the highly developed countries of Europe, and notably of Protestant Europe, there is today a new anti-politics. It is sustained above all, though by no means only, by the young. It involves a turning-away from the state and traditional parties, and insistence on values which are fundamentally different from those of the work society, 'alternative' values. The 'alternatives', as they call themselves, are not necessarily 'green' and certainly not only interested in environmental improvement, though they often sail under this flag. While their political successes may be short-lived, their support is strong and sustained. In some parliaments, they have already upset the traditional coalition games by their blocking minorities. In many countries they signal new concerns which are far removed from the world of production which so preoccupies British politics.

In Britain, even a sensible exposition of such views sounds strangely out of place. If Maurice Ash, in his pamphlet *Green Politics: The New Paradigm*, demands a 'politics of meaning', most people will wonder what he is talking about. Of course it is desirable to fight the soullessness of bureaucratised societies; but few would know what to make of the statement that 'jobs, as such, are part of the structures that alienate us'. Is that a way to fight unemployment? And the notion that 'a politics of meaning does not require permanent political parties', will make most people shake their heads and turn away.[27]

Yet there is something suspicious about this reaction. For one thing, there are changes with which traditional political approaches do not come to grips. Shirley Williams hints at some of them, though even she returns to the work society and traditional production politics. It is perfectly possible that the changes which are happening before our eyes will give the economy, and above all production, a different place in our priorities. They do not become unimportant, to be sure, but they cease to be all-important. Economic stability remains a necessary, but is no longer an overwhelming, condition of human welfare and political success. Perhaps we have already ceased to live in a work society. With these changes, the puritanical streak in British politics loses its point. In fact, British politics is puritanical through and through. There is not one group which advocates the enjoyment of life. They all want hard work, busy fraternal activity, in 'chapel, union and Parliament', at best the 'self-respect' and status of work. Perhaps British politicians would not be ill advised to take a leaf out of Anthony Crosland's dreams of a quarter-century ago. 'Total abstinence and a good filing-system are not now the right signposts to the socialist Utopia.'[28] He might have said, total abstinence, hard work and the right filing-system are not now the right signposts to Britain's future. 'As our traditional objectives are gradually fulfilled, and society becomes more social-democratic with the passing of the old injustices, we shall turn our intention increasingly to other, and in the long run more important, spheres – of personal freedom, happiness, and cultural endeavour: the cultivation of leisure, beauty, grace, gaiety, excitement, and of all the proper pursuits, whether elevated, vulgar, or eccentric, which contribute to the varied fabric of a full private and family life.'[29] And why not?

Chapter Twenty-three
THE ECONOMY, OR WHICH FUTURE WORKS?

For the time being, the main battlefield of debate about Britain and its future is likely to remain the country's economy. If we remove the issue from the polemic of day-to-day politics, it is about one important question: is Britain in fact, 'far from being sick', '. . . transforming the heritage of the industrial revolution' and 'slowly becoming a post-industrial society' with its own kind of viability (as Bernard Nossiter argues in his book *Britain: A Future That Works*[1]), or has Britain 'in essence . . . evolved into a poor man's version of the post-industrial state' which needs a radical change of direction to become viable (as the authors of *The Future That Doesn't Work*, in this case Leslie Lenkowsky, argue in a variety of ways[2])? The difference of view is a convenient starting point for our own summary. This, however, should be said right away: one must beware of misunderstanding the issue of Britain's future, or that of any other industrial country for that matter. Getting the economy right is demonstrably a necessary condition of the improvement of people's life chances, but no more. It is not a sufficient condition, and therefore any programme which confines itself to matters economic is bound to go astray.

The authors of the two books which form our starting point here have one notion in common: that is, that Britain defines in some way the future of the rest. Arguably, this is a mistake which vitiates the remainder of their argument. Whoever proceeds from the general to the particular in this way, is unlikely to find answers which apply to real conditions. Even 'post-industrial society' is too general a term to make much sense for a particular country. Here we shall take the line that Britain is unique, and so is its economic predicament. Britain's economy is certainly linked to the rest; moreover, it certainly shares a number of problems with some others; but any answer has to build on the unique traditions and strengths of the country. Britain's story need not be told to others; in any case, others have no reason to recognise themselves in it; but it has to be told to Britain itself – which is the main intention of this book.

The title of the collection of essays, *The Future That Doesn't Work*, clearly implies that Britain's present represents the future for the rest. But the authors whose contributions R. Emmett Tyrell has assembled find this a future which they would not wish on others. Trade unions, nationalised medicine, the Conservative party and the welfare state have failed, as well as the economy. Moreover, 'intellectuals have consequences'. 'The fish, so the French say, decays from the head first,' as Colin Welch puts it. He has a particular animus against the London School of Economics which for him is the major part of the head of the fish. William Beveridge ('a socialist in all but name'), R. H. Tawney, Graham Wallas, Beatrice and Sidney Webb are some of his targets.[3] But since he attacks them in the name of Friedrich von Hayek and probably of Senator Patrick D. Moynihan and many other LSE advocates of free enterprise and monetary economics, another fish has its head in the same place. The London School of Economics is quite an aquarium, in other words.

Peter Jay suspects a less conspiratorial cause of the disease which he calls 'Englanditis', though he too suggests that the disease might spread. The deep-seated causes of decline which he sees are very serious, for they link prosperity with democracy. 'So we reach the depressing conclusion that the operation of free democracy appears to force governments into positions (the commitment to full employment) that prevent them from taking steps (fiscal and monetary restraint) that are necessary to arrest the menace (accelerating inflation) on which political stability and therefore liberal democracy depend. In other words, democracy has itself by the tail and is eating itself up fast.'[4] Were this true, it would be a serious condition indeed, and also one that is not confined to England. But is it true?

First of all, there are countries which have full employment, little or no inflation, and democratic institutions. They may be small – such as Switzerland and Austria – but they are real. Secondly, it must, as we have seen, be very doubtful indeed whether unemployment can be regarded as an effective, let alone a defensible instrument for bringing down inflation. More than that, the slight deceleration of inflation which Britain has experienced under a policy of fiscal and monetary restraint has by no means helped stabilise political democracy, quite apart from the fact that it has failed to stimulate economic growth. The diagnosis of gloom, of a 'poor man's version of the post-industrial state', is as misleading as the recommendation for unemployment coupled with fiscal and monetary restraint. Britain's economy as it stands today may not work, but its future must look different from the proposals advocated by Peter Jay.

Clearly, the American journalist Bernard Nossiter was annoyed by the prevailing pessimism about Britain, and even more by the particular analysis of R. Emmett Tyrell's volume. His own book, *Britain: A Future That Works*, is in many respects a careful and informative discussion of British politics and society. In the economic part of his analysis, Nossiter looks at the City and other areas of the service industry, and he rightly finds them remarkable. Indeed, he finds them so remarkable that de-industrialisation, for him, becomes a positive gain. Here is the full statement from which portions have already been quoted: 'Far from being sick, the place is healthy, democratic, productive, as stable a society as any of its size in Europe. It is transforming the heritage of the industrial revolution, shedding its plants, the mills and some of the values that made them work. It is slowly becoming a post-industrial society where a decreasing number of men and women are concerned with the production of goods, and an increasing number with things of the mind and spirit – services in the economists' accounting.'[5]

The term 'post-industrial society' is borrowed from Daniel Bell, whose *Coming of Post-Industrial Society* describes the transition from production to services, and notably to sophisticated, often scientific services in the advanced world[6]. Bell is not unaware of the cost of this transition; with respect to liberty and progress, his book is far from optimistic. But an author must accept that his concepts acquire a life of their own; both Leslie Lenkowsky and Bernard Nossiter imply that the post-industrial state is a desirable one. Actually, Nossiter does not think that Britain will, or should, go all post-industrial: 'an advanced society, moreover, will surely keep and expand industries near the frontier of knowledge – nuclear power, micro-electronics, drugs and many more'. Is Britain doing this? Anyway, 'more and more, Britain will earn its way by trading its skill with words, music, banking, education and leisure for the products of more traditional societies'[7].

It is hard to resist the temptation to mention that trading in education has been made virtually impossible by the policies of successive governments which can only be interpreted as attempts to keep overseas students out; in banking there is more and more foreign competition, and in any case little support in the country, as the popularity of the 'windfall tax' in the 1981 budget showed; so far as trading with words is concerned, publishers do not find life easy . . . But the more fundamental point is that Bernard Nossiter's picture of Britain's economy is charmingly, if hopelessly idealistic. It is certainly true that Britain continues to offer certain services at a level of quality, and in a quantity which are unrivalled elsewhere. But it is simply not true that there can be a victory of 'leisure over goods', that is, an alternative between services and manufacturing. The post-industrial society works if manufacturing has shed, first dirt and grime, and then jobs, but in doing so has increased productivity to such an extent that it still provides the economic basis of a country. And in this respect as in others, society and country continue to coincide; there is no international division of labour which would allow one country to provide all the goods, and another, all the services. Thus, Britain's de-industrialisation is a real problem which will have to be solved if Britain's services are to remain as important as they were and are.

This leads to the central issue of economic policy, its objectives. Given the climate of the world economy and the facts of British economic life, it is advisable to be realistic in what one aims for. If Britain maintains its present level of economic activity and perhaps improves it slightly in the years that remain of the twentieth century, this would be a considerable achievement. Not even Japan could produce an economic miracle today. The cost of labour and of oil; the apparent saturation of markets; the immobility of industrial giants, that is to say, the cost of new investment; political uncertainties; growing protectionism; the increasing impoverishment of the poor; and other reasons, make the 1980s very different from the 1950s. It is therefore not an advocacy of zero-growth, but a realistic assessment of economic opportunity, to suggest aiming for stability rather than significant expansion, and being pleased if in fact growth-rates of one per cent per annum or even a little more can be achieved, at least in good years.

Stability does not mean stagnation. On the contrary, the stability suggested here involves major internal shifts. First of all, it requires adjustment in the technical sense of the term. By that is meant the virtual discontinuation of certain industries and the development of others. Here, capital, technology and labour have to be flexible and forward-looking. In the case of labour, adjustment means changing skills and at times, painful though it is for individuals and difficult though it is in view of rigid housing policies, geographical mobility. Stability does not mean that every individual remains where he or she is in terms of income, either. There is a place for a considerable improvement of the position of the poor; many Britons even outside the underclass still do not enjoy the elementary citizenship rights of a civilised society. Moreover, there can and must be plenty of scope for individual achievement.

But the main point is that economic policy and public attitudes must be geared to slow and limited progress. Even this will be hard to attain. In order to achieve stability the first and crucial requirement is confidence. Economic confidence has been mentioned before; but it may be useful at this stage to summarise the main ingredients of this precious commodity. They are at least four.

One is a political environment with built-in shock-absorbers, one, in other words, in which sudden and quick L- or U-turns are avoided. In discussing political institutions, the changes have been listed which would help increase confidence; electoral reform and a bill of rights are the most important. In addition, political leaders must be able to inspire confidence. This is probably a more important quality than anything else. Leadership is to a large extent about confidence and credibility; if these are lacking, the best policies will go to seed.

Secondly, medium and long-term thinking have to prevail, both in politics and in business. In this, the role of the financial institutions is important. But financial institutions do not exist in a vacuum. There has to be a general sense that what matters is stability over a period, rather than profits next year. Some of the hectic quality needs to be taken out of British public and economic life. There really is no point in getting excited over quarterly statistics, indeed over monthly figures about growth and the balance of trade and even unemployment. There is a point in thinking ahead and accepting that as one goes along, there will be valleys as well as peaks, and that encountering a valley is no reason to panic; if anything it is a reason to brace oneself for the climb.

Thirdly, and possibly most controversially, a regular forum for bringing about a common understanding of issues and needs on the part of government, employers and trade unions is inescapably necessary.

This too has been discussed at some length earlier in this book, so that it may suffice to re-emphasise it here. Nowhere is the British sense of solidarity more urgently needed than in the understanding of the parameters of stability. This means assessing the relationship between wages, productivity, profits, investment, and general prosperity. There is a need to gear wages to productivity, and to make sure that profits are invested sensibly. The need is not likely to be satisfied by the market alone. A mixed economy is no market economy, however much one may regret it. Conjuring up the textbook image of a market economy does not change reality. In Europe in particular, collective action, not only by workers, is as much a part of the economic scene as the implicit or explicit guarantee of certain citizenship rights; and this will not change. Given this background, it is hard to avoid the conclusion that ways must be found, and found again, to bring about systematic co-operation between the three corners of the 'corporate triangle'.

The precise institutional form which this takes is a matter for discussion, and for trial and error. Of course it would be desirable not to set up quasi-corporate arrangements, thereby creating a grey area of non-accountability. The closer the arrangements are to the visible structures of government, and to Parliament, the better. But institutional details must not detract from the basic need to find, not so much a consensus – no one should expect intrinsically different interests to disappear or merge into a common view – as a common understanding of problems from which compatible actions are bound to arise. One other point is worth repeating. Every 'social contract' will be broken. Each of the three sides is bound to find certain actions of the others unbearable. But no such breach of contract can ever be a good reason not to try to conclude a new one. After all, the British know better than others that the real world does not comply with categories of Cartesian clarity.

Finally, one of the elements of confidence is the openness of the country to the world. There can be no stability, and no confidence, in isolation. Not only is trade both ways a central plank of economic stability, but it is never sufficient for a country to base confidence in economic stability merely on government and a few large firms who get by whatever happens. A country which closes itself off from the world is bound to be seen by others as anxious, worried, and an unreliable partner for investment and trade. It is therefore bound to go down the slippery path to impoverishment, black markets, administrative regulations, and ultimately probably to a police state which enforces the unenforceable. Again, it is an open question exactly how international economic relations should be organised. There is more 'orderly marketing' than free trade in the world today, and this is not likely to change. But confidently sharing sovereignty is a necessary condition of stability.

These are four formal prerequisites of confidence. They indicate *how* things should be done, not *what* should be done. This is deliberate. What should be done is to a large extent a function of what can be done, and that means of how the relevant arrangements work. Take the not implausible view of the leader writer of *The Economist* that the secret of the conquest of the depression of 1931 was a reduction in real wages, and that if only such a reduction could be brought about, we might well get out of the present economic mess.[8] This is probably true; but it is an effective truth only if those involved can agree on the remedy and accept its consequences. Anyone who tries to reduce real wages by fiat, will, at any rate in Europe, earn a degree of unrest which he or she will not live down. The process has to be gradual and widely accepted to be successful. This means long, boring hours of explanation and negotiation. It means breakdowns of talks and incipient industrial action. But then, it is indefensible for a politician to say that he spends eighty per cent of his time explaining the obvious to ignorant people, and only twenty per cent to governing; the obvious is not equally obvious to all, and whoever loses his patience in explaining what he thinks is obvious will find much time to think about it before long, because he will soon find himself out of office.

What has been said about cutting real wages applies to the various elements of supply-side economics, and of neo-Keynesianism in much the same way. Government is only a part of a complex economic tangle. Indeed, in a sense, government is no more than a catalyst or an arbitrator. Yet in this role it is indispensable. Things may be different in America; they are even different in various European countries; but for Britain the only recipe for confidence lies in something like the four sets of attitudes and arrangements which have been listed; and confidence is the necessary, indeed perhaps the sufficient, condition of stability.

This is not all that there is to say about Britain's economy. The question of how high technology can better be translated into managerial practice, for example, would require a separate argument. Here, the educational system undoubtedly has a task. The question of how the service industries can continue to serve a wide international community rather than just Britain, is equally important. Then there is the question of how conditions can be created under which more people are encouraged to set up their own small businesses, and how those who have done so can be prevented from giving up. But the starting point of it all is the question of how to arrest the process of de-industrialisation. It is here that the objective of overall stability or modest growth, and the instruments of confidence, have their place.

All this does not add up to a very exciting political programme. It has an air of *déjà vu* about it, and while in fact Britain keeps on repeating the same old mistakes, it does not like repetition in words. However, the very familiarity of the character of the recipes here proposed makes them appropriate. They build on Britain's experience, and they therefore have a chance of working. They rely on values for which Britain has been known, and which have made Britain strong. Above all, they put the economy in its place, and a place which Britain has accepted in the past while others gave it more prominence. This is not to be misunderstood. It is not us who put the economy in its place, but a changed world socio-economic climate, and the advances which all industrial countries, including Britain, have made in recent decades. Still, a stable economy is the beginning of a return to its basic virtues by a country which is envied by many. It is the basis of a future for Britain that might work.

Chapter Twenty-four
A BRITISH FUTURE

For the participant observer of the British scene, few things are more bewildering than the extent to which the public debate is preoccupied with yesterday's world. Politicians and authors alike, and even journalists, seem bent on re-writing British history rather than looking forward to the future. Some wish that Britain had had an economic miracle, and so try to bring it about at a time at which few things are less likely. Others want Britain to have had at least a decade of benevolent Keynesianism mixed with social generosity and economic prosperity, but fail to see that this is an approach from the past, which is spent even where it succeeded. Again others still hanker after socialism, when the failure of all its versions to improve human welfare has become evident decades ago. Few recognise that the world has changed, that modernity has run into contradictions and new ways forward have to be found. In this respect, too, Britain has opted out of the mainstream of debate and of action.

This is a pity. While it may be argued that thinking around production and the development of the work society makes rather more sense for Britain than for the leaders of the world league table of economic success, it is just conceivable that new issues have come to the fore to which Britain has better answers than the rest. This is where the British tradition may help shape a better future. Britain's strength lies not in replacing goods by leisure, but in adding to economic stability a dimension of human improvement.

What this means can best be explained in terms of a central problem of yesterday, today, and tomorrow: that is, work. By work is meant here what people do in their jobs, occupations or professions. Work is crystallised human action, hardened into highly defined posts in factories, offices, organisations. Work in this sense was the centre of people's lives in yesterday's world. As a general medium of life, such work is a modern invention; for most, the lines between living and working were blurred in pre-industrial circumstances. It is only in the last century or so that one came to be forced to have a job in order to survive. Promptly, the whole of society was built around jobs. They not only provided people with the necessary earnings, but were also the basis of social entitlements in the welfare state, and of course determined people's self-respect. Who are you? means more often than not: what are you doing? This in turn does not mean that one is reading or eating or otherwise enjoying oneself, but that one has a job. In the work society, people seem to exist only in so far as they have a job to define their position.

And Britain is a work society. Shirley Williams illustrates this involuntarily when she says that there is not 'much evidence that, once offered a reasonable job, people prefer leisure. Work instills self-respect; it is a means of defining who one is and what one can attain. A world without work would be one in which most people would be profoundly unhappy, bored and purposeless.'[1] Yet, could it not be that this, too, means hanging on to a world which no longer is? Is not Hannah Arendt right when she says that the work society is running out of work?[2]

There are some striking observations which apply to Britain as they do to other industrial countries. Since 1918, working lives have been cut on average by about two-thirds. Shorter working hours, longer initial education, earlier retirement, longer holidays will conspire to that end. Nevertheless, unemployment is rising all over the industrial world. There are very few countries in which there are not at least five per cent unemployed, and several in which the figure is higher than ten per cent. Among young people it is in any case very much higher. Another ten per cent or so are, as one might put it, voluntarily unemployed; they are in educational establishments of one kind or another, or are women who would like to have a job but do not register as unemployed. Of those who remain in employment, many are underemployed. There is barely an employer who could not achieve the same output with ninety per cent, eighty per cent, or even seventy per cent of the present workforce. From the point of view of employees, underemployment is the curse of the age; having a job without enough to do is more humiliating than conveyor belt work has ever been. Whereas in the past, new inventions have invariably created new jobs along with the old ones which they destroy, it now appears as if technology and organisation permit an economy which can dispense with a great deal of human labour. One must not overstate such developments; but even a conservative assessment is bound to conclude that unless we change our attitudes, unemployment will remain at ten per cent at least, and perhaps become much higher.

Changing our attitudes, however, does not mean returning to yesterday's world. Here and there, a job creation scheme may make sense; but by and large such schemes are but expensive attempts to camouflage real changes. They create new underemployed; that is, they humiliate people in the name of self-respect. There is one exception, though it leads into rather controversial territory. Clearly, one of the reasons why we are running out of jobs is cost. Wherever possible, expensive labour has been replaced by cheaper machines. In some areas, however, expensive labour has not been replaced by anything. This is true above all in the personal services, but also in environmental work in the widest sense. If we want these things done – as we should – there is no way in which the present labour market can cope. What is necessary is that people give some part of their lives, a year perhaps, to the community, in order to make sure that the quality of the lives of all remains high. Some kind of community service, in other words, is a necessary condition of welfare.[3] It is not a competitor of a Youth Opportunities Programme, nor of a system of apprenticeships and vocational training. These are answers of the work society, which may be necessary but do not solve the problems of tomorrow.

To return to the mainstream argument, there clearly are not enough jobs to go around, nor will there be in the foreseeable future. What is to be done? Here, a distinction is in order which is as old as it is important: the distinction between work and activity. Work is human action that is heteronomous, imposed by external needs, be they needs of survival or of power. Activity, on the other hand, is human action which is freely chosen, which offers opportunities for self-expression, which carries its satisfaction within itself, which is autonomous. Aristotle saw the difference, though he chose to distinguish between the 'practical' and the 'theoretical' life; more than two thousand years later, Karl Marx introduced the terminology here adopted. It enables us to make sense of the fact that while our societies may be running out of jobs, they are certainly not running out of work in the conventional sense. There is enough to do, enough also for people's self-respect and to give meaning to their lives. One of the central issues of the world of tomorrow is the transformation of work into activity, and more generally, the expansion of the role of activity in people's lives.

The distinction between work and activity is not to be misunderstood. There is no necessary incompatibility between the two. Some people find that their jobs offer them opportunities for activity. Perhaps the habit of concentrating on social problems has made us overlook how far this is true for how many. In other cases, jobs can be so transformed that they offer chances of activity. What has come to be called the humanisation of work, is a major issue of social policy. Not only the world of production, but above all that of services is badly in need of an enlargement of the scope for human expression and initiative. Work need not be heteronomous, an imposed and unwanted burden, if we put our minds to bringing about the necessary changes.

In the nature of the case, activity will be the dominant characteristic of people's lives outside work. Leisure is an unfortunate term. It carries within it the whole burden of the work society. Leisure means that people recover from work and gather strength for further work. The more important point is that when one leaves one's job, there is plenty of scope for activity. One can do things, rather than just relax, sit about and become a spectator. One can even accept tasks which used to be, and for some still are, work. The black economy is an area of activity, perhaps because the rules which govern work do not apply. The black economy is also something else. It is a testimony to the fact that what we are arguing here is not primarily a programme for government action, but one for people themselves. More than that, people already do what we are preaching. As the world of work has contracted, people have increasingly looked for other outlets for their talents and energies. It may well be that people do not prefer leisure, but that they prefer activity. Their self-respect is quite often determined by achievements other than those of their jobs. They are by no means unhappy, bored and purposeless. But of course – they have their jobs to begin with. We are still talking about the other side of the coin of the work society. It will take much time, and major breaks with established habits, to create a society of activity. How, for example, do people earn their living if not in jobs? On what basis are taxes levied? How are the entitlements of social policy determined? In any case, what do people do all day?

There are answers to these questions, but they should be left in suspense here. The point of this apparent excursion into fantasy – into an 'alternative' world – was to demonstrate that there are changes which one cannot cope with by looking back. All the palliatives which Britain's political parties offer will not come anywhere near dealing with the problems of tomorrow. Thus the parties will fail. The work society will linger on, at least in official thinking and acting, but the activity society will have its way one day. For the future is bound to catch up, even with a Britain so set in ways which it has never really liked.

This is the second reason why the question of work was raised in a book on Britain's decline and possible upturn: it is quite wrong to stare at official pronouncements and the stilted debates of yesterday's men and women. What matters is what happens where people live and work and play. There, the changes at which we have hinted are evident. What is more, with respect to these changes, Britain is in a surprisingly strong position. If I was asked what I regard as the main opportunities of the next twenty years, if one wants to advance the cause of liberty in the rich countries of the world, I should mention three: the transformation of work into activity; the growth of new social ligatures; the strengthening of the market society. In all three, the traditions and realities of Britain promise greater success than most other rich countries can hope for.

On work and activity, little needs to be added to what has already been said. To avoid misunderstanding, however, it should be stressed that in the short run, there is obviously a case for maintaining and even creating jobs. What is needed is the opening-up of opportunities for activity at the same time. These are in part formal, such as generous allowances for early retirement; in part substantive, such as incentives for work humanisation; and in part an almost natural result of the shrinking of jobs. In the medium term however, more drastic measures will be inevitable. It will not, for example, make sense to translate increases in productivity invariably into higher earnings. If this is done, a new two-class society of rich employed and poor unemployed will develop still further, and the ensuing battles might be quite disagreeable. What will be necessary is the translation of some of the gains in productivity into time. Higher output enables people to have more time off, that is, more time for activity. The important point about all this is, however, that even today many people in Britain treat their work as activity. What may be a disadvantage in terms of productivity, the fact that people work to live rather than living to work, is a step in the direction of a society of activity.

For ligatures, an analogous case can be made. Much has been made of the issue of social cohesion, because it is one of the keys to people's life chances, especially in a modern society. People get satisfaction out of seeing their options embedded in the co-ordinates of belonging. Shirley Williams has put this in simple and lovely words when she talks about human beings being 'made whole again', and about 'a sense of belonging, of being cared for, of being wanted, of being part of a network of relationships with people and also with objects'.[4] Much of this is still alive in Britain. Some of it has, on the other hand, crumbled. It is not very likely that the ligatures of tomorrow will be the same as those of yesterday, that is, family and locality, church and class in the old sense of these notions. But they may be built on similar lines; in any case they will have to build on small units. Social cohesion is never just the cohesion of a total society. Unless this is mediated by numerous smaller units, it will fall apart at the slightest prompting. Again, it would be wrong to venture too far into the realm of speculation. It is hard to tell what exactly people's lasting ties will look like in ten or twenty years' time. But once again it is likely that Britain will find it easier to nurture such ties, because in order to do so, all people need to do is connect their future with the experiences of their recent past.

The third and most critical opportunity for liberty tomorrow has been implied and even made explicit in connection with the other two. In simple words, it is that what matters is not governments but people. Governments cannot do very much to advance human liberty. They can guarantee the basic rules of living together, and the citizenship rights of all including a decent standard of living for the old, the infirm, the disadvantaged. This, governments will have to continue to do, unless we want to risk the very basis of a free society. But above and beyond these elementary needs, governments must withdraw from our lives. 'Less government' is a very pertinent political demand, though it must not be misunderstood as a free pass to cut services which are needed to back up the citizenship rights of all. Less government means above all more initiative by, and autonomy for, individuals, groups, businesses, organisations, decentralised units of all kinds. This is what I mean by the term 'market society'.

For some strange reason, the word 'market', has become a term of abuse in some quarters. There is the belief that a market economy tends to strengthen the strong and weaken the weak. Perhaps the same suspicion would accompany the use of the wider term 'market society'.

Governments, it is thought, have the job of ironing out the injustices brought about by the market. They must redistribute resources and power. In so far as generalised citizenship is concerned, this is certainly correct. Nothing that has been said here can be read as a plea to neglect the underclass, the poor, the disadvantaged. Unless full participation in the life of society is regarded as a right for all, liberty remains an empty phrase, even a smokescreen behind which privilege thrives. But it does not follow from the definition of a minimum of rights of participation and the demand that government should be the guardian of a society of citizens, that we must rely on government throughout. Both in the economy, and in wider social matters, governments tend to disturb and deflect the desires and initiatives of people. Ultimately, the interests and wishes and dreams of individuals and the concerns of small units are a very much better guide to greater welfare for all than big government can ever be. Trust in decentralised units, and above all in individuals, is, however, trust in the market, that is, in the free interplay of autonomous forces and its beneficial effects.

Britain has a peculiar history in this respect. It has lost its market economy a long time ago. Nationalisation, economic policy, and the sheer size of important 'private' enterprises have led to a condition for which there are many names – oligopolistic, interventionist, mixed economy, and the like – but not one of them includes the word 'market'. It is not very likely that this will change significantly in the years to come, though one would hope that in some areas of economic activity at least the chances for initiative and competition will grow. At the same time, Britain has remained to a significant extent a market society. In many areas, self-regulation is preferred to government control. The autonomy of institutions which has been listed as one of the strengths of Britain at the very beginning of this book, remains pronounced. Voluntary organisations of many kinds play a major role. The fact that government in Britain is not present in all spheres of life, already there every time the individual comes puffing along, is of inestimable importance. In this respect too, Britain can build on its past, whereas others have to undo centuries of *étatisme*, of state domination, to reach even the starting point of a market society.

There are many reasons for the widespread distrust of government and of the parties which sustain it, and quite a few of them are good reasons. Big government has arrogated to itself more and more functions, and at the same time it has become increasingly unable to breathe life into anything. But many people draw inconsistent conclusions from this insight. Some are past masters at wishing the withdrawal of government for others while insisting that they of course must be spared. Others seem to think that government itself should cut back its influence and encourage initiative. This, however, is not the way things happen. They are either done by people and groups themselves, or not at all. Government has to be ignored, until its irrelevance is for everyone to see. Once again, this is possible in Britain, where at least one does not have to ask the government for permission if one wants to ignore it. Let a hundred flowers bloom, then, and Britain will find itself again!

Man does not live by bread alone. Certainly, man needs bread to live. Economic stability is the first item on the agenda of Britain's future. It requires an effort by all; and it is not a task for government alone, or even primarily for government. The century-long slide has to be arrested. The best way to do so is by remembering the British virtues of solidarity and co-operation. A country which inspires confidence in investors and buyers and the public of the world generally, has already won half the economic war. This Britain can do, and must do. But Britain must not become so preoccupied with bread that it forgets its virtues, and the values for the sake of which we work and eat. The first item on the agenda of the future is not necessarily the most important one. Economies are never a purpose in themselves. As we get to those ingredients of human welfare and life chances for which economic stability is merely a necessary, and not a sufficient, condition, we discover in Britain's past and present a great deal of strength. Whether Britain shows the way to others or not, is immaterial; but there is a British way ahead which can give much satisfaction to people at home. This road has to be taken by the people themselves. They may join forces, create organisations, build localities, set up enterprises, but they must not wait for anyone else to tell them what to do. On the contrary, the leash of government has to be pulled and pulled until it gives. A network of relationships which holds people, and a full life of activity which gives them satisfaction, are two objectives of which sight must not be lost. Britain has long been a remarkably happy country. It can remain that, if it remembers its strengths and applies them to the issues which have upset its equilibrium for a period.

NOTES

NOTES

I want to thank Belinda Giles for helping to identify and assemble material used in several chapters of this book, and for her assistance with these notes.

Chapter One
A Personal Preface

1 George Mikes: *How to Be an Alien* (Wingate: London/New York 1946).
2 Ralf Dahrendorf: 'Aus der Bettperspektive', in *Inselmenschen*, ed. by Fritz von Woedtke (Axel Springer: Hamburg 1948).
3 George Mikes: *op. cit.*, p. 44.
4 Sidney Webb in a letter to the Rt. Rev. Archibald Robertson in 1903 about a visit to Sir Owen Roberts in 1895. See Sydney Caine: *The History of the Foundation of the London School of Economics and Political Science* (G. Bell & Sons: London 1963).
5 Wieland Europa (Ralf Dahrendorf): 'Plädoyer für ein Zweites Europa', in *Die Zeit*, 2 July and 9 July 1971.
6 See *Proceedings of the European Parliament*, No. 641, September 1971; p. 80 *et seq.*
7 Ralf Dahrendorf: 'Not By Bread Alone', in *Financial Times*, 30 Dec. 1976.

Chapter Two
Decline Without Fall

1 Martin Wiener: *English Culture and the Decline of the Industrial Spirit, 1850–1980* (Cambridge University Press: Cambridge 1981); p. 28.
2 Quoted from John Stuart Mill's *Principles of Political Economy* by Martin Wiener: *op cit.*, p. 33.
3 Friedrich Engels: *The Condition of the Working Class in England in 1844*.
4 Alexis de Tocqueville: *Journeys to England and Ireland*, 1835.
5 1895: Michael G. Mulhall, *Industries and Wealth of Nations*. 1977: *Economic Outlook*, No. 27 (OECD July, 1980).

6 Report by the Commission on the Depression of Trade, 1885–6. Final report, p. 106.
7 Alfred Marshall: *Industry and Trade* (Macmillan, 1919).
8 See T. C. Barker: 'L'Economie Britannique de 1900 à 1914 – Declin ou Progres?', in *Revue d'Histoire Economique et Sociale*, vol. 52, no. 2, (1974).

Chapter 3
The Strengths of Weakness, the Weaknesses of Strength

1 Thus Marx in the Preface to his *Capital*.
2 Title of the book by the American author, Bernard Nossiter (see ch. 21).
3 See, e.g., George Gallup: 'What Mankind Thinks About Itself', in *Readers Digest* CIX (October 1976).
4 Werner Sombart: *Warum gibt es keinen Sozialismus in den Vereinigten Staaten* (1906); trans. *Why is there no Socialism in the United States?* (Macmillan: London 1976).

Chapter 4
Decline and (Almost) Fall

1 See Walt W. Rostow: *The World Economy* (Macmillan: London 1978); ch. 17.
2 Samuel Brittan: 'How British is the British Sickness?', in *The Journal of Law and Economics*, vol. xxi (Oct. 1978); p. 246.
3 Peregrine Worsthorne: 'The Right Way to Cure Our Racial Ills', *Sunday Telegraph*, April 2, 1981.
4 See Shirley Williams: *Politics Is For People* (Penguin Books: Harmondsworth 1981); ch. 11.
5 Peter Jay: 'Englanditis', in *The Future That Doesn't Work*, ed. by R. Emmett Tyrell, Jr., (Doubleday: Garden City, N.Y. 1977); p. 167.

Chapter Five
The Vanishing of the Industrial Spirit

1 Samuel Brittan: 'How British Is the British Sickness?'; in *The Journal*, etc. p. 247.
2 Martin Wiener: *English Culture*, etc.; p. 170.
3 Peter Jay: 'Englanditis', in *The Future, etc.*; p. 169.
4 See Martin Wiener: *op. cit.*; p. 113.
5 Quoted from Ruskin's *Works* by Martin Wiener: *op. cit.*; p. 39.

6 Quoted from R. H. Tawney's *The Acquisitive Society* by Martin Wiener: *op. cit.*; p. 115.
7 *R. H. Tawney's Commonplace Book*, ed. by J. M. Winter and D. M. Joslin (Cambridge University Press: Cambridge 1972); p. 75.
8 Eric Hobsbawm: *Industry and Empire: An Economic History of Britain Since 1750* (Weidenfeld and Nicolson: London 1968); p. 142.
9 *R. H. Tawney's Commonplace Book*; p. 75.
10 Quoted from R. H. Tawney's *The Acquisitive Society* by Martin Wiener: *op. cit.*; p. 115.
11 *R. H. Tawney's Commonplace Book*; p. 53.
12 Quoted from E. M. Forster's *Two Cheers for Democracy* by Martin Wiener: *op. cit.*; p. 72.
13 See Martin Wiener: *op. cit.*; p. 13.
14 See n. 7, Ch. 2 above.
15 John H. Goldthorpe, David Lockwood, Frank Bechhofer, Jennifer Platt: *The Affluent Worker* (Cambridge University Press: Cambridge 1968).
16 Nancy Mitford: *The English Aristocracy* (from *Noblesse Oblige*, ed. A. S. C. Ross, Hamish Hamilton 1956).

Chapter Six
A Matter of Inequality?

1 Peter Bauer: *Class on the Brain – The Cost of a British Obsession* (Centre for Policy Studies: London 1978); pp. 1, 2.
2 Royal Commission on the Distribution of Income and Wealth: *Reports* No. 1, 4, 7, 8; Cmnd 6171 (1975).
3 A. H. Halsey: *Change in British Society* (Oxford University Press: Oxford 1978); p. 42.
4 John Goldthorpe: *Social Mobility and Class Structure in Modern Britain* (Clarendon: Oxford 1980).
5 Peter Bauer: *op. cit.*; p. 9.
6 Peter Bauer: *op. cit.*; p. 10.
7 Frank Field: *Inequality in Britain: Freedom, Welfare and the State* (Fontana Paperbacks 1981); p. 66.
8 Shirley Williams: *Politics Is For People*; p. 36.
9 Peter Bauer: *op. cit.*; p. 9.

Chapter Seven
The Upper Classes, or How the Tone is Set

1 The paper was the *Neue Zürcher Zeitung* in August 1981.

2 Jilly Cooper: *Class – a View From Middle England* (Eyre Methuen: London 1979). Her 'dramatis personae' appear on pp. 11–12.

3 Michael Young: *The Rise of the Meritocracy* (Thames & Hudson: London 1958).

4 Richard Hoggart: *The Uses of Literacy* (Chatto and Windus/Penguin Books: London 1958); ch. 10.A.

5 Richard Hoggart: *op. cit.*; p. 294.

6 Richard Hoggart: *op. cit.*; p. 302.

7 Bernard Nossiter: *The Future That Works*; p. 180.

Chapter Eight
The Working Classes, or How Things Hold Together

1 Jilly Cooper: *Class etc.*; p. 63.

2 See Richard Hoggart: *The Uses of Literacy.*; ch. 3.

3 Richard Hoggart: *op. cit.*; pp. 80, 81.

4 Richard Hoggart: *op. cit.*; p. 72 *et seq.*

5 Edward Shils: 'British Society', in *The Sociology of Modern Britain*, ed. by Eric Butterworth and David Weir (Fontana/Collins 1970); p. 498 *et seq.*

6 *Fifth Report from the Home Affairs Committee, 1980–81* (House of Commons Paper 421 – I).

7 *The Brixton Disorders 10–12 April 1981.* Report of an Inquiry by the Rt. Hon The Lord Scarman O.B.E. HMSO 1981. pp. 109, 110.

8 Michael Manley: 'A Paradox for the Creatures of Empire', *The Guardian*, July 21, 1981.

9 Karl-Heinz Bohrer: 'Babylon brennt', *Frankfurter Allgemeine Zeitung*, July 25, 1981.

Chapter Nine
Does Class Matter?

1 A. H. Halsey: *Change in British Society*; pp. 43, 45.

2 Samuel Brittan:'How British Is The British Sickness?' in *The Journal, etc.*; p. 6.

Chapter Ten
A Place of Strife

1 Charles K. Rowley: 'The Economics and Politics of Extortion', in *Trade Unions: Public Goods or Public 'Bads'* (Institute of Economic Affairs:

London 1978); p. 91 *et seq.*

2 'An Industrialist': 'The wonder is there aren't even more strikes', *The Daily Telegraph*, January 18, 1979.

3 Peregrine Worsthorne: 'The Trade Unions: New Lads On Top', in *The Future That Doesn't Work*; pp. 7, 9, 11.

4 Cyril Grunfeld: 'Union Law and Power: Current Issues', in *Trade Unions: Public Goods etc.*; p. 82.

5 Committee of Inquiry on Industrial Democracy: *Report*, HMSO 1977.

6 Samuel Brittan: 'How British Is the British Sickness?'; in *The Journal, etc*; p. 7.

7 Keith Middlemas: 'Trade Unions: The Case for Self-Discipline', in *The Times*, August 5, 1981.

Chapter 11
The Westminster Game

1 S. E. Finer, ed.: *Adversary Politics and Electoral Reform* (Anthony Wigram: London 1975); p. 3.

2 S. E. Finer, ed.: *op. cit.*; p. 6.

3 S. E. Finer, ed.: *op. cit.*; p. 13, p. 16.

4 T. Wilson: 'The Economic Costs of the Adversary System', in S. E. Finer, ed.: *op. cit.*; p. 103.

Chapter Twelve
Short-Term Thinking

1 T. Wilson: 'The Economic Costs of the Adversary System', in S. E. Finer: *Adversary Politics and Electoral Reform*; p. 103.

2 Harold Lever and George Edwards: 'How to Bank on Britain', *The Sunday Times*, 9 Nov. 1980.

3 See ch. 9 of the *Report* of the Committee to Review the Functioning of Financial Institutions (1980).

Chapter Thirteen
A Corporate Bias

1 See Richard Rose: The Problem of Party Government (Macmillan: London 1974).

2 Keith Middlemas: *Politics in Industrial Society: the Experience of the British System Since 1911* (Andre Deutsch: London 1979); p. 15.

3   Keith Middlemas: *op. cit.*; p. 243.
4   See T. H. Marshall: *Citizenship and Social Class* (Cambridge University Press: Cambridge 1950).
5   Keith Middlemas: *op. cit.*; p. 18.
6   Keith Middlemas: *op. cit.*; p. 423sq.
7   Keith Middlemas: *op. cit.*; p. 450.

Chapter Fourteen
London and the Rest

1   S. E. Finer: *Adversary Politics and Electoral Reform*; p. 18.
2   George Jones and John Stewart: 'Why the Local Council Hatchet Job Is So Unfair', in *The Times*, 14 August 1981.

Chapter Fifteen
The Politics of Economic Decline

1   Richard Rose: *The Problem of Party Government* (Macmillan: London 1974); p. 313sq.
2   James E. Alt: *The Politics of Economic Decline. Economic Management and Political Behaviour in Britain Since 1964* (Cambridge University Press: Cambridge 1979); p. 112.
3   James E. Alt: *op. cit.*; p. 157.
4   James E. Alt: *op. cit.*; p. 184.
5   James E. Alt: *op. cit.*; p. 231.
6   James E. Alt: *op. cit.*; p. 261.
7   James E. Alt: *op. cit.*; p. 247.
8   James E. Alt: *op. cit.*; p. 270.

Chapter Sixteen
Some Steps Forward

1   Michel Crozier, Sam Huntington, Joji Watanuki: *The Crisis of Democracy* (N.Y. University Press: New York 1975).
2   For the following presentation, see M. Steed: 'The Evolution of the British Electoral System', in S. E. Finer, ed.: *Adversary Politics and Electoral Reform*. The quotation from George Goschen is on p. 41.
3   Michael Steed: *op. cit.*; p. 53.
4   Nevil Johnson: 'Adversary Politics and Electoral Reform – Need We Be Afraid?', in S. E. Finer, ed.: *op. cit.*; p. 89.

5 See *Report* of the Hansard Society Commission on Electoral Reform (June 1976).
6 A survey of different methods to attain consensus can be found in Ralf Dahrendorf, ed.: *Trendwende: Europas Wirtschaft in der Krise* (Munich 1981).
7 All quotations from Keith Middlemas: 'Trade Unions: the Case for Self-Discipline', in *The Times* 5 August 1981.
8 Leslie Scarman: *English Law – The New Dimension* (Stevens & Sons: London 1974); p. 61 *et seq.*
9 *English Law and Social Policy* (Centre for Studies in Social Policy: London 1975); p. 42 *et seq.*
10 Leslie Scarman: *op. cit.*; p. 15.
11 *English Law and Social Policy*; p. 7.
12 *English Law and Social Policy*; p. 36.
13 Ruling by the European Court on 13 August 1981.
14 See *English Law and Social Policy*; p. 35 *et seq.*

Chapter Seventeen
A Question of Identity

1 *Hansard*, vol. 823, 28 October 1971; cols. 2187, 2189.
2 Tony Benn: *Arguments for Socialism*, ed. by Chris Mullin (Jonathan Cape: London 1979); p. 95.
3 William Wallace: *The Illusion of Sovereignty* (Unservile State Papers No. 24; Liberal Publications Department 1979); p. 1.
4 William Wallace: *op. cit.*; p. 9 *et seq.*

Chapter Eighteen
Post-Imperial Britain

Chapter Nineteen
Special Relationships

1 Winston Churchill: *A History of the English-Speaking Peoples*, vol. 4 (Cassell: London 1958); p. xi.
2 Winston Churchill: *op. cit.*; p. 254.
3 Karl Heinz Bohrer: *Ein bisschen Lust am Untergang. Englische Ansichten* (Hanser Verlag: Munich 1979); p. 133.

4 Karl Heinz Bohrer: *op. cit.*; p. 129.
5 Karl Heinz Bohrer: *op. cit.*; p. 135.

Chapter Twenty
The European Dilemma

1 Andrew Shonfield: *Europe: Journey to an Unknown Destination* (Allen Lane: London 1973).

Chapter Twenty-one
Britain in the 1980s

1 James Bellini: *Rule Britannia. A Progress Report for Domesday 1986* (Jonathan Cape: London 1981); p. xv.
2 Karl Heinz Bohrer: *Ein bisschen Lust am Untergang. Englische Ansichten* (Hanser Verlag: Munich 1979).

Chapter Twenty-two
Models of Britain

1 Ian Gilmour: *Inside Right. A Study of Conservatism* (Quartet Books: London 1977).
2 David Lipsey and Dick Leonard, eds.: *The Socialist Agenda. Crosland's Legacy* (Jonathan Cape: London 1981); p. 1.
3 Nigel Forman: *Another Britain* (Bow Group Publications: London 1979); pp. 6, 7.
4 Keith Joseph and Jonathan Sumption: *Equality* (John Murray: London 1979); p. 1.
5 Keith Joseph and Jonathan Sumption: *op. cit.*; p. 23.
6 Keith Joseph and Jonathan Sumption: *op. cit.*; p. 61.
7 Keith Joseph and Jonathan Sumption: *op. cit.*; p. 11.
8 Tony Benn: *Arguments for Socialism*. Edited by Chris Mullin. (Jonathan Cape: London 1979); p. 146.
9 Tony Benn: *op. cit.*; p. 44.
10 Tony Benn: *op. cit.*; p. 48.
11 Tony Benn: *op. cit.*; p. 53.
12 Tony Benn: *op. cit.*; p. 84.
13 Tony Benn: *op. cit.*; p. 179.

14 Tony Benn: *op. cit.*; p. 139 *et seq.*
15 David Owen: *Face the Future* (Jonathan Cape: London 1981); p. 3.
16 Shirley Williams: *Politics Is For People*; p. 16.
17 David Owen: *op. cit.*; p. 55.
18 David Owen: *op. cit.*; p. 359.
19 David Owen: *op. cit.*; pp. 357, 358.
20 Shirley Williams: *op. cit.*; p. 69.
21 Shirley Williams: *op. cit.*; p. 45.
22 Shirley Williams: *op. cit.*; p. 125.
23 Shirley Williams: *op. cit.*; p. 72.
24 Shirley Williams: *op. cit.*; p. 89.
25 Shirley Williams: *op. cit.*; p. 97.
26 Shirley Williams: *op. cit.*; p. 98.
27 Maurice Ash: *Green Politics: The New Paradigm* (The Green Alliance: London 1980); pp. 14–17.
28 Anthony Crosland: *The Future of Socialism* (reissue Jonathan Cape: London 1980); p. 357.
29 Anthony Crosland: *op. cit.*; p. 353.

Chapter Twenty-three
The Economy, or Which Future Works?

1 Bernard Nossiter: *Britain. A Future That Works* (Andre Deutsch: London 1978); p. 196.
2 Leslie Lenkowsky: 'Welfare in the Welfare State', in *The Future That Doesn't Work*; p. 162.
3 Colin Welch: 'Intellectuals Have Consequences', in *The Future That Doesn't Work*; p. 60.
4 Peter Jay: 'Englanditis', in *The Future That Doesn't Work*; p. 181.
5 Bernard Nossiter: *op. cit.*; p. 196.
6 Daniel Bell: *The Coming of Post-Industrial Society* (Basic Books: New York 1973).
7 Bernard Nossiter: *op. cit.*; p. 197.
8 *The Economist*, Vol. 280, no. 7201.

Chapter Twenty-four
A British Future

1 Shirley Williams: *Politics Is For People*; p. 76.
2 See Hannah Arendt: *The Human Condition* (Doubleday: New York 1959).

3 See my Preface to Enrico Colombatto: *Nation-Wide Social Service: A Proposal for the 1980s* (Centre for Labour Economics, London School of Economics, Discussion Paper No. 84, December 1980).

4 Shirley Williams: *op. cit.*; p. 45.